Books by Joni Eareckson Tada . . .

Joni
A Step Further
When Is It Right to Die?

All GOD'S Children

Ministry with Disabled Persons

Gene Newman
Joni Eareckson Tada

ZondervanPublishingHouse
Academic and Professional Books
Grand Rapids, Michigan

A Division of HarperCollins*Publishers*

Requests for information should be addressed to:
Zondervan Publishing House
Academic and Professional Books
Grand Rapids, Michigan 49530

Library of Congress Cataloging in Publication Data
Newman, Gene.
    All God's children : ministry with disabled persons / Gene Newman, Joni
Eareckson Tada. — Rev. ed.
        p.   cm.
    Includes bibliographical references.
    ISBN 0-310-59381-6
    1. Church work with the handicapped. I. Tada, Joni Eareckson. II. Title.
BV4460.N48   1993   92-28627
259'.4—dc20   CIP

Cover design: John M. Lucas

Printed in the United States of America

93 94 95 96 97 / CH / 9 8 7 6 5 4 3 2 1

To Dr. Sam Britten,
with gratitude for his spiritual leadership
and his unending concern for the disability community

Contents

Acknowledgments

This book was first developed as a seminar syllabus while I was employed by ACAMPAR Programs, Inc. Because of the increasing demand and need for a publication of this nature, the ACAMPAR Board of Trustees gave Joni and Friends, Inc. the publication rights for *All God's Children*. It was the prayer of the ACAMPAR Board of Trustees that *All God's Children* would be a practical tool for pastors and church workers interested in ministering to the disability community.

I want to express my gratitude to the ACAMPAR Board of Trustees for their encouragement to develop a resource guide of this nature. A special thank-you is also in order to Pat Hamman for his support, leadership, optimism, and commitment to excellence. Camille Beckham, Vesta Bice, Donna Hall, Linda Harry, Nena Huston, B. J. Maxson, DeAnn Sampley, and Lynne Seno need to be commended for their efforts in producing this revised edition.

Many others have played a part in the development of *All God's Children*. Their faithful labors were indeed a manifestation of the dynamic and unified church of the Lord Jesus Christ. These individuals (too numerous to list here) will receive their just reward when they hear their Savior's words, "Well done, good and faithful servant."

Finally, I want to express my appreciation to Monique, my wife and co-laborer. Without her help, this project would never have come to fruition.

Gene Newman

Preface

There I was, out of the rehab center only a few weeks, sitting upright and awkward in my bulky wheelchair and wondering what to do about Sunday morning. I knew my church had been praying for me since my diving accident two years earlier in 1967, but facing people terrified me. Would they stare? Would I know what to say? Would I have to sit next to my family in the pew, half blocking the middle aisle? And what if I had to wheel into the rest room—would I fit?

What I discovered that Sunday morning, after my family lifted me out of the car and into my wheelchair, changed my entire outlook on church. Someone had hammered together a few pieces of plywood to make a ramp. People smiled and asked me how I was doing at college. Old friends asked me to sit with them and held my Bible and hymnal. The feeling was warm and friendly. I felt welcomed. I belonged.

Joni Eareckson Tada

What happened in Joni's little church can happen in any congregation. That's what JAF Ministries is all about. And that is why you hold *All God's Children* in your hands. Our hope is that churches across the country will become better equipped to minister to persons with disabilities. This manual is filled with motivational, inspirational, and instructional helps designed to assist you and your church in preparing and conducting disability ministry.

Disability ministry can be as small as helping a family such as Joni's when she was first injured—as one-on-one as a smile, a makeshift ramp, and a place to sit in a worship service. Or disability ministry can be structured as an entire department that organizes outreach to groups of deaf, mentally handicapped, blind, or physically disabled persons. Whether small or large, the goal is to create awareness, become responsive, and reach out with the love of Christ.

CREATING AWARENESS

At the beginning of the book you will learn about the way God views handicapping conditions. His sovereignty and his purposes concerning disabilities highlight this section. Next, you will discover the role the pastor and volunteers play in creating awareness. And awareness is what is first needed before you plan an outreach—it is all part of preparation.

BECOMING RESPONSIVE

After surveying your church to discover what the needs are in your church community, you will learn how to address those needs. It may mean making a few buildings or even programs more accessible. It may mean a new class in your church's Sunday school. Addressing needs may involve securing new equipment and supplies such as large-print Bibles or hearing loops in one of the pews. Becoming responivse to the disabled people God has placed in your church fellowship will lay the foundation for further outreach.

REACHING OUT

When your church is finally prepared, you will then be able to conduct disability outreach to new families or even institutions such as deaf schools or residential centers for people in wheelchairs. Your church's outreach can be as large (or as small) as spiritual and practical resources allow. But the foundational steps are critical: Before you can reach out, a church needs to become aware and responsive.

All God's Children is designed to be used wherever you and your church are in the process. It is a tool to help pastors motivate their congregations. It is a guide for teachers to become motivated to minister to disabled persons. The sections containing resource information can help you in researching needs and creating a network with other ministries. Whether yours is a small congregation with a plywood ramp or a large church with a bus service to local nursing homes, *All God's Children* will help motivate, inspire, and instruct Christians who want to demonstrate God's love to and with disabled people.

Our prayer for you is from Isaiah 6:8: "Here I am. Send me." God has a work for you, just as he had one for Isaiah. And like Isaiah, may he prepare you and lead you. The result? Your life will be enriched, disabled people will be reached, and God will be glorified.

Introduction

The World of Disabilities ... or Is It Handicaps?

WHICH WORDS DO WE USE?

And now to those words—the words that make you squirm and wince, groping for the right language to use when meeting a person who, through illness or injury, is different from you. I make it a practice to look through brochures and literature from other organizations that serve the disability community, and I am amazed at the variety of words that are used to describe a person's condition or disease. It confuses even me.

In an admirable effort to dispel the social stigma that surrounds words such as *crippled* or *invalid*, some groups have coined contemporary phrases to underscore the positive perspective. There are those who prefer to call us "handi-copeable" or "handicapable." We are the "physically challenged" or the "mentally challenged." To some, we are the "special people." To others, we are the "physically exceptional."

My friend, Gloria Maxin, who happens to be disabled (or "challenged," if you prefer), has written an exposé that pokes fun at the baggage of words our society has invented about our limitations:

> I've had a hard time accepting these modern euphemisms for various handicaps, such as "hearing impaired," "language impaired," "vision impaired," "motion impaired," etc.

Hmm, I wonder if the immoral will soon be called the "spiritually impaired." Oh, I hate such words because they sound squeamish. I hear in them a horror to say and see our simple reality. They're Mother Hubbard words clapped around our nakedness with missionary zeal to make us respectable—and to cover our shame. So I much prefer the tough Old Testament words like "deaf," "dumb," or "crippled" that tell the plain truth and set us free. Yet I'm a hypocrite of sorts. I'll refer to my plain fat with such euphemisms as "imposing" or "robust" or "substantial."

She has a point. In our great care to do away with prejudice in our semantics, perhaps we end up drawing more attention to the situation than we would have had we stuck with a good old honest word like *disabled* or *handicapped*.

Yet, are there valid differences and shades of meaning between even these two words? Dictionaries will tell us that "disability" is a word commonly used to describe a lack of physical or mental ability. "Handicaps," on the other hand, are any encumbrances that make success more difficult to attain.

Robert Lovering, a man disabled by polio, describes these differences in his book *Out of the Ordinary*.

I can conclude that I am always disabled, but I am not always handicapped. When I was a whole person and played basketball, being only six feet tall was a handicap, but I was not disabled. Working at my desk in my wheelchair I am not handicapped unless you ask me to reach a book on the third shelf over my desk. Therefore, in my condition, I am only handicapped when I try to accomplish something in which my disability makes success more difficult. Does the term really matter? I am what I am.[1]

And people are who they are—individuals who happen to have a disability. People are not to be labeled "retards" or "cripples" or "handicaps." They are people who happen to have a physical or mental impairment that may or may not handicap them as they go about their daily routines.

WHAT DOES IT MEAN TO BE DISABLED?

Somebody once said that although our bodies may disable us, it is often society which handicaps us. A disease or an impairment—light seizures, loss of vision, the loss of a hand or leg, a progressive condition such as arthritis or MS, mental retardation, or brain or spinal injury—can present problems. Yet many people control or at least manage their disabilities with either therapy, treatment, medication, or adaptive equipment.

However, these same people, with anything from annoying to chronic disabilities, may be severely handicapped if they lack an attendant or family member who can help with daily care routines. Handicaps occur when these same people are denied access due to steps or curbs, lack of elevators, ramps, Braille signs, or interpreters. One is handicapped by the attitudinal barriers of pity and fear. Even lack of transportation or employment, housing, or finances can present a handicap to the disabled person who desires to live independently. And, like members of the able-bodied community, disabled people are handicapped by sin.

You and your church can help persons with disabilities manage their way through a world of handicaps, freeing them to stretch beyond their limitations. People with impairments are whole people with desires and dreams, opinions and interests, vices and virtues. Life, full and rich with potential, is within the grasp of persons with disabilities.

You can help those who are disabled step beyond their handicaps.

Joni Eareckson Tada

Speed

Just as the dawn speeds through the night,
And dreams give way to morning light
(Which seemed so real before my sight)
So with the day I see and feel
Things which are true, joys that are real.
And when the shadows creep around,
These things won't flee, they will abound;
Because the truth of things is found.

Doris Dodge

Doris Dodge has cerebral palsy. Poem used by permission.

I

God Does Not Create Accidents

THE QUESTION OF "WHY?"

Ask anyone who has been awakened out of spiritual slumber with an ice-cold splash of suffering. "Why?" is often the question. "Why me, Lord?"

In reality, those few words are rarely spoken out of a heart that is honestly searching for answers. Initially, the question may be voiced in resentment, bewilderment, or frustration. A person recently diagnosed with a disabling impairment or a progressive disease may clench his or her fist in anger against God.

There may come a time when these same people search through Scripture trying to discern the real purpose behind everything that has happened. Sometimes, though, they are compelled to face a verse like Romans 11:33: "Oh, the depth of the riches of the wisdom and knowledge of God! How unsearchable his judgments and his paths beyond tracing out!"

OUR UNDERSTANDING IS FINITE

J. I. Packer, in his book *Knowing God*, tackles this problem of our inability to understand the purposes of God behind every event.

Now the mistake that is commonly made is to suppose that
the gift of wisdom consists in an ability to see why God has
done what He has done in a particular case, and what He is
going to do next. . . . People feel that if they were really
walking closer to God, so that He could impart wisdom to
them freely, then they would discern the real purpose of
everything that happened to them. . . . If they end up
baffled, they put it down to their own lack of spirituality.
Such people spend much time wondering why God should
have allowed this or that to take place. . . . Christians may
drive themselves almost crazy with this kind of futile
inquiry.[1]

What makes us think that even if God explained his ways to
us, we would be able to understand them? It would be like
pouring million-gallon truths into our one-ounce brains. Even
the great apostle Paul admitted that, though never in despair, he
was often perplexed (2 Cor. 4:8). One Old Testament author has
written, "As you do not know the path of the wind, or how the
body is formed in a mother's womb, so you cannot understand
the work of God, the Maker of all things" (Eccl. 11:5).

Yet, even though "there are secrets the Lord your God has
not revealed to us" (Deut. 29:29, LIVING BIBLE), we are never
lacking hope. There is an answer.

GOD IS SOVEREIGN

Let God's own words to Moses speak for themselves: "The
LORD said to him, 'Who gave man his mouth? Who makes him
deaf or dumb? Who gives him sight or makes him blind? Is it not
I, the LORD?' " (Exod. 4:11). And hear the words of Jeremiah the
prophet: "Is it not from the mouth of the Most High that both
calamities and good things come?" (Lam. 3:38). The Psalmist
says, "For you created my inmost being; you knit me together in
my mother's womb. . . . My frame was not hidden from you
when I was made in the secret place. When I was woven together
in the depths of the earth, your eyes saw my unformed body. All
the days ordained for me were written in your book before one of
them came to be" (Ps. 139:13, 15–17).

Scripture indicates that not only is God sovereign to physical injuries or illness, but he is Lord over the changes and alterations that transpire within the womb.

Does this mean that God wants disease and injury? The key here is how we use the word *want*. God doesn't want disease to exist in the sense that he *enjoys* it. He hates it just as he hates all the other results of sin—death, guilt, sorrow, and catastrophes. But God must want disease to exist in the sense that he *wills* or *chooses* for it to exist. If he didn't, he would wipe it out immediately.

So God is neither frustrated nor hindered by Satan's schemes, but he permits suffering to serve his own ends and accomplish his own purposes.

THERE IS A PURPOSE

Although suffering is largely a mystery, it is not a mystery without direction. God has his reasons. Whether it is to mold Christian character, to stimulate empathy toward others who hurt, to refine one's faith, or to focus one's attention on eternal glories above, only time and wisdom will tell. The whole ordeal of our suffering is inspired by God's love. We are not the brunt of some cruel, divine joke. God has reasons, and learning some of them can make all the difference.

The following story vividly illustrates how God often uses the most unlikely candidates to accomplish his will. It is written by Gloria Hawley, the mother of two mentally retarded children.

Psalm 127:3 speaks of children as a "gift of the Lord" and "a reward." I didn't disagree with God, I simply refused the thought. Gradually, gently, God's light began to invade the particular dark chamber in my mind. Finally I realized that all biblical principles apply to all people. Each individual must respond, by an act of his will, and apply the principles to his situation. So I determined to administer large doses of God's Word to Laura and Craig.

They seemed bored, so I began to sing Scripture to them. Craig became helpless with laughter, while Laura smiled politely and put fingers in her ears. It became apparent that the children needed the Scripture to be related to their own personal frames of reference.

Laura and I began with the 23rd Psalm. "Jesus is Laura's strong Friend and Protector. He takes care of her in a very special way. Laura cannot see Him but He sees her. She is His darling little lamb."

The paraphrase delighted and animated Laura. Her large, soft, brown eyes glowed and sparkled. Her smile was dazzling. Her attention span stretched as her understanding was kindled.

A miracle occurred.

Her teacher sent a note home: "Laura is so animated; she is singing and telling the other youngsters, 'I love you, kids! I love you!' "

Her speech therapist called: "What are you doing with Laura? She is responsive and bubbly!" My explanation was met with a cautious silence. Then—"If it works, do it. Send the Scripture along, and we'll work on it here too."

This shy, silent, fearful daughter of ours had begun her ministry—to teach me; to exhibit God's power; to bring God's Word into other lives.

Laura particularly liked the end of the Psalm which, for her, stated: "And some day Laura will go to live in Jesus' house and be with Him all the time! They will talk together, and she'll be able to tell Him how much she loves Him. No one will have to say it for her—she will be able to say it herself! Laura will live with her special Friend, Jesus, all the time. They will talk and sing and laugh together—with love. . . ." Psalm 23 is Laura's special Psalm.

A few weeks passed and Christmas was near. Craig loved the story from Luke 2. Enthusiastic and responsive, he received the Baby Jesus with gusto. The miracle repeated itself.

Craig's teacher called and, in tears, described how he had told his class about Jesus' birth—the star, God's love, angels and shepherds.

Our little boy, his eyes shining with the light that split the heavens so long ago, spilled over with God's message of unchanging love—to a group of abnormal children no one had thought to tell before.

Craig's ministry had begun.

Craig and Laura remain handicapped. God has not chosen to 'heal' them. He is pleased to use them.[2]

Joni Eareckson Tada

Box 257

For all of us who are handicapped
I hope you will remember us.
Remember us talking outside and having fun.
Remember the man who can't see, laughing and joking.
Don't ignore us.

When we make friends we hold them in our minds
And remember the happiness we had.
Sometimes we make friends and for ten days,
*   or nine weeks, or longer, we are close*
But then it's funny how you forget us
While we remember you.

Sometimes the light goes out and you turn your back on us.
And I feel like a toy in a box.
Box 257, or 258.
You take out and play with me and talk to me
But there are no real feelings of love.
Nine weeks, and then "Goodbye, back in your box,
*   I have new friends now for another nine weeks!"*

What now for all of us?
Do you want us just to sleep and leave you alone
In our box on the top shelf?

John Hunt Kinnaird

John Hunt Kinnaird is a quadriplegic owing to brain damage at birth. He lives in southern Chester County, Pennsylvania. Poem copyright © 1981 by John Hunt Kinnaird. Used by permission.

II

Tremendous Possibilities

A MATTER OF PERSPECTIVE

How should the church respond to disabled individuals? We could respond with despair, depression, and a sense of hopelessness, or we could view these people as the catalysts of great opportunity. The examples below demonstrate how one church seized the opportunity offered by disabled individuals and turned pity, fear, and avoidance into empathy, quest, and involvement.

THREE SUCCESS STORIES

What do a young man on a motorcycle, a woman talking on the phone, and a man moving chairs have in common? Plenty. All three of these people have been eternally changed as a result of their involvement in one church's Special Ministries Department. Meet my friends Rodney, Debbie, and John.

Rodney

Rodney is a young man with Down syndrome, a condition characterized in part by mental retardation. He has been involved in a special Sunday school class for several years. One day after church I encountered Rodney, and we started to chat. Our conversation went something like this:

"Hi, Rodney. How are you doing?"

"Better than last week."

"What happened last week?"

"I came to church for the night service. After church, I got on my motorcycle, but it ran out of gas before I got out of the parking lot."

"What did you do then?"

"I walked the motorcycle down the street to the gas station, but it was closed. So I pushed the motorcycle all the way to another gas station that was far away. When I got there, it was closed too."

"Rodney, that was terrible! What in the world did you do?"

"Well, I got up on my motorcycle and started to pray. A few minutes later, a man in a car stopped and drove me to a gas station."

When Rodney told me this story, I was deeply touched. The living God was having an impact on his life. Instead of crying or panicking, he climbed on his motorcycle and simply trusted his Savior.

Debbie

Debbie has faithfully served in her church's Special Ministries Department for several years. In addition to being a highly organized, efficient, personable, and godly woman, Debbie is physically disabled. As a young girl she contracted polio, which left her quadriplegic with only partial use of her arms.

Debbie's ministry represents an important principle that should undergird every disability ministry, that is, *our disabled friends should not only be ministered to, but also be permitted to minister their gift to the body of Christ.* Debbie's gift of administration and exhortation has had a dramatic impact on the congregation of her church. I hasten to add that, as a result of her ministry, Debbie has not only touched many lives, but also she has developed the self-esteem and dignity that comes through participation in the Lord's work. Additionally, by laboring alongside her able-bodied brothers and sisters, Debbie's physical differences have become less apparent, and her spiritual and nonphysical similarities have become increasingly visible.

John

John is a successful businessman who became involved in disability ministry as part of a "package deal." His two teenaged boys wanted to work with the mentally handicapped, and Dad reluctantly tagged along.

John demonstrated his fear and ignorance one day when he stated, "I'll help arrange chairs and do some of the administrative work, but don't expect me to actually work with these people."

Over the next several months God did a wonderful work in John's heart. He began to see past his students' physical and intellectual imperfections, and he began to view them through God's eyes. John graduated from arranging chairs to teaching. He discovered that God gave him love, concern, and empathy for these special brothers and sisters.

A couple of years later, John rearranged his working schedule so he could have every Wednesday off. He started a Bible study at a nearby home for physically disabled young people and even developed a curriculum to teach them the fundamentals of Christianity.

John's story demonstrates how our Lord can take a self-centered and lukewarm Christian and mold him into a choice servant.

IN THE FISHBOWL

A ministry to the disability community affords the church a wonderful opportunity to display God's magnificent, unconditional, and impartial love before the watching world. This truth is borne out by the experience of Grace Community Church of Sun Valley, California, which has developed a large Special Ministries Department.

This Special Ministries program was the subject of a radio interview with John MacArthur, the senior pastor of the church. The talk show host, who had attended Grace Church, was overwhelmed to find such a large number of disabled persons in the congregation. But he was even more impressed, he said, to discover how people with disabilities are accepted by the leadership of the church. "Just the fact that they are there is one thing," he said. "But when the people in leadership embrace them, touch them, and talk to them . . . that's impressive, because you just don't see that." It goes without saying that if the leaders of the church show this kind of acceptance, it's easier for the other members to do so.

I find it fascinating to see how God can take a ministry to the "unlovelies" and turn it into such a visible, concrete, and powerful display of his love. The apostle Paul, in his letter to the church at Corinth, expressed it well when he wrote, "But God chose the foolish things of the world to shame the wise; God chose the weak things of the world to shame the strong" (1 Cor. 1:27).

In his book *Three Steps Forward, Two Steps Back*, Charles Swindoll eloquently supports this position.

> We're all faced with a series of great opportunities brilliantly disguised as impossible situations.[1]

Discerning the opportunities behind the disguise is the challenge facing those who desire to establish disability ministry.

My mind has doors, and I was afraid to open them.
But when I did, I saw old friends.
Hurt, Love, Fear and Depression.
I said "Hello" to them and then
"Get off my back!"
But they didn't listen.

One of these friends comes when I am sleeping.
His name is Hurt.
Hurt says, "Think of girls."
And then he leaves my mind.

"Hello, Fear. What are you doing here?"
"I'm making you afraid to speak to girls."
"How do you do that?" I ask.
"When you look in their eyes you'll see pity
And hear it in their voices
And so you won't talk to them of love."

Now here comes Love to say "Hello."
"What do you do?" I ask.
"I give love to men and women, boys and girls
But they don't want to give it back to you."
And then Love says, "Okay. I'll give you friends
But they'll only tease you and walk out on you."

And so again I sleep, and with the morning
Come my friends to say hello once more.
"Friends, I'm fighting back. You can't control my thoughts.
I have strong medicine to help . . . Jesus."
He is listening, seeing, loving and helping me.
I speak to Him and He answers with what is best for me.

John Hunt Kinnaird

III

The Role
of the Pastor

A SHEPHERD'S TASK

The demands placed on most pastors are ever increasing. Consequently, when presented with the proposition of initiating a new program, a pastor's response will very likely be, "I think it is a worthwhile program, but I simply do not have the time."

Can this dilemma be resolved? Can a new ministry be initiated without adding one more burden to the already overworked pastor?

This problem is not new, of course; it has plagued the church since its inception. In Acts 6 it is recorded that the infant church was increasing in numbers so rapidly that the apostles could not continue to meet the needs of the congregation. Verse 2 tells us that the apostles summoned the congregation and said, "It would not be right for us to neglect the ministry of the word of God in order to wait on tables." Does that statement sound familiar? The apostles knew that their commission was to teach the Word of God; however, if they were to "wait on tables" (serve food to the widows), they would have to change their priorities.

The apostles resolved the matter by telling the church to appoint seven Spirit-filled men to be responsible for the distribution of food. This allowed the apostles to give themselves

continually to prayer and to the ministry of the Word (Acts 6:4).
John MacArthur, in his book *The Church: The Body of Christ*, has
commented on this decision:

> The apostles were not being proud or lazy. They were not
> above visiting people. But they were establishing a priority
> for their own ministry. They saw that their distinct contribu-
> tion to the Body was not menial activity, but praying and
> teaching the Word to equip the saints for the ministry.[1]

The pattern established in Acts 6:1–4 is monumental. God
knew that a pastor could not possibly meet all the needs of his
flock by himself; he needed help. The help comes from Spirit-
filled saints.

The apostle Paul presents the same pattern in Ephesians
4:11–12: "It was he who gave some to be apostles, some to be
prophets, some to be evangelists, and some to be pastors and
teachers, to prepare God's people for works of service, so that
the body of Christ may be built up." Paul is saying that a pastor
can maximize his time by training Christians to carry out their
own ministries.

John MacArthur has stated:

> Why do gifted men equip the saints? So that they might do
> the work of the ministry. The gifted men are to teach the
> Word to equip the saints to do the work. Teaching is the
> pastor's job.
>
> Too often, however, this biblical pattern is thwarted by
> church members who expect pastors to do everything. No
> wonder some pastors suffer so much physical and emotional
> fatigue. Some have been driven to breakdowns—they can't
> find the time to study the Word of God—because their
> church members expect them not only to equip the saints,
> but to do the work of the ministry also. That is not God's
> plan for the body.
>
> The local church essentially is a training place to equip
> Christians to carry out their ministries. Unfortunately, for
> many Christians the church is a place to go to watch
> professionals perform and to pay the professionals to carry
> out the church program.[2]

What can we conclude from this discussion of equipping?
Several points can be delineated regarding the shepherd's task:

1. **Equip**   The busy pastor can maximize his time by teaching God's Word. This will equip the flock to do the work of the ministry.

2. **Inform**   If a pastor determines that there is a need for a ministry with disabled persons, he should inform the congregation.

3. **Pray**   The need must be committed to the Lord through prayer.

4. **Wait**   If it is God's will for a ministry with the disability community to be undertaken, he will allow a leader to emerge from within the congregation. *It is important to wait for the right leadership.*

A SHEPHERD'S PERSPECTIVE

Because of its exceptional ministry to disabled persons, Grace Community Church serves as a model for other churches considering this kind of outreach. Pastor John MacArthur's responses to commonly asked questions are most instructive:

Question: How did you view handicapped individuals prior to the development of your church's Special Ministries Department?

Answer: When I was in junior high school, I had a very close friend who was disabled. He was kind of spastic—I don't know the clinical term—but he always dragged one foot behind him and had to have special shoes. He was just mobile enough to want to participate in sports, but the other kids didn't want him on the team. The girls didn't know what to make of him, either; they just looked at him as kind of funny. But that boy and I were very, very close friends. He would stay at my house, and I'd stay at his.

That friendship did two things for me: first, it gave me a sensitivity to disabled people, and second, it removed the stigma of disability. Our relationship was also very significant in that I gained some valuable insights in helping him work through a lot of his anxieties.

This guy was my first contact with a disabled person, and after that, I never had any particular misgivings about disabled people.

Question: Did you have any fears or concerns about starting the Special Ministries program at your church?

Answer: No fears at all. I felt that this was a tremendous thing from the very start. After all, in his Word the Lord says, "When I have a banquet, these are the people I want to invite." It's his feast, his invitation. He doesn't leave anyone out, so why should we? You know, this kind of ministry takes you out of the cosmetic world where everything is perfect. These are real people with real needs just like everyone else.

Question: What are the benefits and liabilities of a disability ministries program?

Answer: I have to be honest with you: I don't see any liabilities. Our disabled members give so much more than they receive from us. For example, when you see them sitting in wheelchairs and you know they've overcome all kinds of obstacles to get to church to worship God, you have to pray, "Thank you, Lord, for my health." They generate an appreciation for so many things the rest of us take for granted. And disabled people help us develop compassion—they make us want to make some active response to their need. They're the personification of "the little ones" our Lord spoke about in Matthew 18.

Question: Why should a church start a disability ministry?

Answer: First, disabled individuals are people made in the image of God. Forget the physical or mental disabilities. They are people made in the image of God—that's all. They are no less marred and no less capable of restoration than his other creations. Second, there is a biblical mandate that we not prefer one over the other. And third, the church is called to reach out to the poor, the needy, the destitute, and the hurting. If we believe the Bible, we have to carry out its dictates. But I don't see it as "grit your teeth and do what's right." I see it as a tremendous privilege. I think these people add a dimension of richness to the whole church family.

Question: How would you counsel the pastor who is considering starting a disability ministry?

Answer: In the first place, considering whether or not to start a Special Ministries program is a little like deciding whether or not a church ought to reach out to lost people. Deciding is really not the issue. As Christians, we have no choice. And if you try to second-guess whether you have the ability to handle it, you'll talk yourself out of it. God knows the needs of the church as well as your own strengths and weaknesses. You have to step out in faith, commit the ministry to the Lord, and believe it is right. If you do, God will supply the people and the resources and will send the Enabler alongside.

Question: With so many different kinds of disabilities and so many hurting people, where do you begin?

Answer: That question reminds me of a poster that we used to have in our church. It read: How Do You Feed a Hungry World? . . . One at a Time! Trying to figure out how your church could feed everyone in the world could cause mass panic! Just take one at a time. Start with your church families, including extended families, and you will likely find many disabled individuals among them. We've seen that happen over and over at Grace Community Church.

Question: What should the role of the pastor be in a disability ministry?

Answer: If the pastor is not completely committed, and if he isn't modeling his concern, it is going to be very difficult to get the people to minister to this population. I don't want to overstate my part, but when a visitor sits next to a guy who grunts and groans and maybe doesn't smell too good, he needs to see that the minister isn't uptight. Sometimes we have complaints about that kind of thing, and if a pastor isn't committed to obeying the Lord, then the pressure may become overwhelming. The pastor has to care about special populations because it is right to care. Then all of a sudden, you care because you care.

Make me a servant
  humble and meek.
Lord, let me lift up
  those who are weak.
And may the prayer
  of my heart always be,
"Make me a servant,
  Make me a servant,
  Make me a servant today."

IV

The Role
of the Volunteer

When I was in the hospital, struggling to piece together the puzzle of my suffering, I desperately needed to know that the Bible was not avoiding the issue of my pain. Now, you'd think that God would have brought my way some smartly dressed, good-looking youth director to grab my attention and get me into God's Word. But no, the Lord had me spend time with another kid my age—a young boy with the spiritual gift of teaching.

Spiritual gifts are God's way of linking his body in love and action. "There are different kinds of service, but the same Lord. There are different kinds of working, but the same God works all of them in all men. Now to each one the manifestation of the Spirit is given for the common good" (1 Cor. 12:5–7).

This boy, Steve Estes, used his gift to start me searching through Scripture and on to a life of meaning and hope. But other people used their gifts—unique energizings of the Holy Spirit—to inspire me further. The list of these gifts is found in Romans 12. But the list of people who can demonstrate the gifts is much longer.

The *gift of mercy* is one of those behind-the-scenes gifts, often administered away from the public eye. It's the lady armed not only with her Bible, but with a box of Kleenex, ready to console the lonely or comfort the hurting. It's that person who will touch or share a hug—who will sit and listen and pray.

During those lonely, fresh-out-of-the-hospital days of early adjustment, I remember one girlfriend who, during visits, would occasionally lie next to me in bed, hold my hand, and sing hymns to me. She didn't give me advice or a grocery list of Bible verses. My merciful friend simply used her spiritual gift.

Does somebody in your church have the *gift of service?* People who have the time, talents, and abilities can be the "hands and feet" of those who are disabled. One might drive a disabled neighbor to a medical appointment or on a shopping excursion. Perhaps the mother of a handicapped child needs a hand with all the extra household chores. A handyman with a heart to serve could construct a ramp or widen a doorway.

Let me give an example. When I was first injured, neighbors would often call my mother and say, "Look, I'm on my way to the market. Have your list ready, and I'll be glad to pick up your items." These people didn't wait for my mother to call them. Instead, they started using their spiritual gifts right away. Curiously, people like that didn't have an inkling as to how to push a wheelchair. They simply wanted to help.

People who have the *gift of administration* have the ability to envision success for those who are often too weak to envision it for themselves. They break down big goals into small tasks and, in the final analysis, enjoy seeing all the pieces come together.

For instance, I never dared to dream of going to college. Being newly disabled, there were just too many obstacles to overcome. Thankfully, another friend of mine used her managing skills to arrange for transportation to and from campus, volunteers to assist with note-taking, and students to escort me from one class to the next. I even needed someone to feed me at the school cafeteria. With the help of my friend and her special gift, I managed life on a college campus and, at the same time, dispelled many fears about venturing into public.

People with disabilities can benefit greatly when others use their spiritual *gift of giving.* Adaptive equipment is very expensive because it may consist of new parts for wheelchairs, braces and crutches, seat cushions, arm splints, Braille typewriters, TTY telephones for the deaf, hearing aids, or canes. Government cutbacks in programs that assist those who are disabled have brought these special needs to the attention of the private sector. By pooling free-will offerings, the church can demonstrate God's love in action by meeting financial needs of disabled persons.

Pastors who have the *gift of prophecy* can rally the rest of the congregation to use their gifts in this unique avenue of service to disabled persons. Lay leadership is much needed, but motivation and inspiration must come from the pulpit.

First Corinthians 12:25 says, "There should be no division in the body, but . . . its parts should have equal concern for each other." And yes, disabled people have spiritual gifts too. Those who are blind, deaf, or mentally or physically disabled don't always have to be on the receiving end. We want to give to the church. I see my place in the body of Christ as one who exhorts and encourages others. Many people have used their gifts to help me; I, in turn, desire to reach out to them.

Although I have the *gift of exhortation*, I don't consider myself a shining example. To exhort others does not mean you're some faultless, plaster saint. A successful use of any spiritual gift presupposes the inability to be perfect. That way we may be sure that God's power will be perfected through our weakness.

You have a spiritual gift too. "Now you are the body of Christ, and each one of you is a part of it" (1 Cor. 12:27). Yet, with all these various spiritual gifts, there are some built-in difficulties. Different people will have different solutions to any number of problems. For example, somebody with the gift of mercy might want to sympathize with a disabled friend, while another with the gift of teaching might want to "sock it to him" with Scripture. One wants to console; another wants to convict.

How do people with various gifts function together in harmony? Paul explains in 1 Corinthians 12:31, "You should set your hearts on the best spiritual gifts, but I will show you a way which surpasses them all" (paraphrase). Then Paul begins his famous "Love Chapter," chapter 13, explaining how love will make it all work. "Patiently looking for a way of being constructive, not impressing or cherishing ideas of your own importance, using your gift with good manners, not pursuing a self advantage, not being touchy" (paraphrase). Truly, Jesus Christ is glorified when his body exercises its gifts in love.

A world of people needs your assistance. And in a real way, you need that world of people. If we are to see the body of Christ at work in the world, all of us—able-bodied and disabled alike— must use our gifts. For our good and the good of others. For God's glory.   *Joni Eareckson Tada*

V
Mental Retardation

More Than a Name

Have you ever played the word association game? Sure you have. Someone says, "Up." You respond, "Down." Let's play.

Word	Response
Tall	_____
Pretty	_____
Happy	_____
Mentally retarded	_____

What is your response to the terms "mentally retarded" and "developmentally delayed"? If you were playing the game, the "right" answer is obviously "giftedness" or "genius." But life is not a game and, unfortunately, through the years I have heard and seen some distressing responses to that term. Some feel that mentally retarded people are mentally ill, deranged, lunatics, or sex maniacs. These misconceptions are the result of a general lack of understanding about mental retardation.

A more accurate response to the term "mentally retarded"

would be "love." People with mental retardation are characterized by a tremendous capacity to love others. Their love is simple, and it is not contingent on reciprocation. It is the love of which Jesus spoke when he said, "Greater love has no one than this, that one lay down his life for his friends" (John 15:13). Certainly many of us can learn a great deal about love from our mentally retarded friends.

Did you pass the word association test? If not, you should spend a few minutes reading this section.

DESCRIPTION

Definition

The dictionary definition of mental retardation is "the lack of powers associated with normal intellectual development, resulting in an inability of the individual to function adequately in everyday life." In lay terms, mentally retarded individuals are "slow learners."

Causes

Mental retardation is caused by

- Genetic defects
- Prenatal influences (disease, trauma, etc.)
- Perinatal influences (birth injuries, premature birth)
- Postnatal factors (disease, environmental deprivation, trauma, poisoning, etc.)

Classifications

The mentally retarded population is categorized under three major classifications:

- Educable
- Trainable
- Profound

Statistics

About 3 percent of the population of the United States is considered to be mentally retarded.[1]

	Educable	Trainable	Profound
Abbreviation:	EMR	TMR	Profound
IQ Range:	51–70	36–50	Below 35
Percent of Retarded Population:	89%	6%	5%
Description:	Able to learn, slow progress	Able to learn self-help skills, socialization, and simple household chores	Gross retardation, minimal capacity for learning
Academic achievement:	Can learn to read, write, do math computations	Can learn to recognize his/her own name, may be able to print name and address	May respond to minimum or limited training in self-help
Social achievement:	Can learn to live independently in a community	Can learn to behave properly, cannot live independently	Limited social skills
Occupation potential:	Can work in jobs requiring limited cognitive skills	Sheltered workshop	Requires complete care and supervision

Misconception

Mental retardation is not synonymous with mental illness and should not be confused with mental illness.

CHARACTERISTICS

Educational

A mentally retarded person generally has the following characteristics:

- Is easily distracted
- Reasons poorly
- Cannot grasp generalizations and abstractions
- Is confused by complexity
- Learns slowly

Physical

Mental retardation, characterized by limited cognitive ability, is often accompanied by physical problems as well.

- Poor motor coordination
- Heart disease
- Seizure disorders
- Visual impairments
- Hearing loss

The health histories of each mentally retarded participant must be reviewed, and appropriate attention given to those with physical problems.

Behavioral

The following behavioral characteristics are common among mentally retarded individuals:

- Short attention span
- Low frustration tolerance
- Lack of modesty
- Childlike mannerisms
- Normal sexual drives
- Normal emotional needs
- Interests that correspond to mental age, not necessarily chronological age

THE CHURCH

Why should the church minister to retarded persons?

1. **We are commanded to love.**

"A new commandment I give you: Love one another. As I have loved you, so you must love one another" (John 13:34).

2. **We are commanded to teach.**

"Therefore go and make disciples of all nations, baptizing them in the name of the Father and of the Son and of the Holy Spirit, and teaching them to obey everything I have commanded you" (Matt. 28:19–20).

3. **Salvation is possible for the retarded person.**

Eighty-nine percent of the retarded population is in the Educable category. Many of these people have reached an age of accountability.

4. **Abundant life is promised the retarded person.**

"I have come that they may have life, and have it to the full" (John 10:10).

5. **Parents of retarded persons need respite care.**

Parents will need times when they are free from the burdens imposed by a disabled child.

6. **Social adjustment for the retarded person is commanded.**

"Train a child in the way he should go, and when he is old he will not turn from it" (Prov. 22:6).

Many years ago a physician (under the influence of the Holy Spirit) wrote:

"When you give a luncheon or dinner, do not invite your friends, your brothers or relatives, or your rich neighbors; if you do, they may invite you back and so you will be repaid. But when you give a banquet, invite the poor, the crippled, the lame, the blind, and you will be blessed. Although they cannot repay you, you will be repaid at the resurrection of the righteous" (Luke 14:12–14).

God's Plan

God's plan for mentally retarded persons is found in his Word. A careful study of the Bible will reveal answers to such questions as (1) Can they learn about God? (2) Are they held accountable? (3) Will God protect them? The following answers are not intended to be exhaustive; rather, they offer some preliminary insights.

1. Can retarded persons learn about God?

God can use the weak.

> "But God chose the foolish things of the world to shame the wise; God chose the weak things of the world to shame the strong" (1 Cor. 1:27).

God does not show partiality.

> "Then Peter began to speak: 'I now realize how true it is that God does not show favoritism but accepts men from every nation who fear him and do what is right'" (Acts 10:34).

> "For God does not show favoritism" (Rom. 2:11).

The Holy Spirit discerns spiritual truths.

> "God has revealed it to us by his Spirit. The Spirit searches all things, even the deep things of God. For who among men knows the thoughts of a man except the man's spirit within him? In the same way no one knows the thoughts of God except the Spirit of God" (1 Cor. 2:10–11).

God's Word will not return void.

> "So is my word that goes out from my mouth: It will not return to me empty, but will accomplish what I desire and achieve the purpose for which I sent it" (Isa. 55:11).

2. Are retarded persons held accountable for their spiritual status?

Accountability is determined by an intellectual awareness sufficient to comprehend salvation.

> "Let the little children come to me, and do not hinder them, for the kingdom of God belongs to such as these. I tell you the truth, anyone who will not receive the kingdom of God like a little child will never enter it" (Luke 18:16–17).

Those who remain like young children will not be held accountable.

Statistics show that 89 percent of retarded people fall into the Educable category. They will reach a peak mental age of nine to thirteen years of age; therefore, it is quite possible they will reach an age of spiritual accountability.

3. Will God protect those who are retarded?

God has promised to protect His "special children."

"Do not exploit the poor because they are poor and do not crush the needy in court, for the Lord will take up their case and will plunder those who plunder them" (Prov. 22:22–23).

HINTS

When working with mentally retarded persons, the following principles should be used:

1. **Success**	Provide successful experiences. Those who experience success will be more willing to try new activities.
2. **Individualization**	Gear activities, lessons, and so on to the level of the individual.
3. **Simplicity**	Give simple and concise instructions. Complex commands will be confusing for the retarded person.
4. **Brevity**	Plan activities for a shortened attention span. If proper activities and materials are utilized, a longer duration of attention will result.
5. **Examples**	Use concrete examples. Abstract discussions should be avoided.
6. **Repetition**	For maximum retention of a concept, use repetition. Repetition aids in impressing facts and ideas upon the brain.
7. **Reinforcement**	Offer reinforcement immediately after a correct response is given. Verbal praise is generally the best reinforcement.
8. **Consistency**	When a proper behavior is exhibited, always praise the person. When an improper behavior is demonstrated, always correct the individual.
9. **Input**	Use a multisensory approach to teaching whenever possible, including the senses of hearing, vision, and touch.
10. **Firmness**	Be firm and loving. Retarded persons often need to be encouraged to participate in activities.

11. **Expectations**	Set the same standards of conduct as for nondisabled persons. *We do not help them by tolerating improper behavior.*
12. **Touch**	Communicate love and approval through hugs and pats. Most mentally impaired persons desire physical contact and will often respond to touch more readily than to words.
13. **Involvement**	Higher functioning persons can serve as helpers. They will feel challenged by the responsibility.
14. **Encouragement**	Allow retarded individuals to do things for themselves as much as possible.
15. **Prayer**	When praying with mentally retarded persons, use short, simple phrases. Ask them to repeat each phrase after you.

NEEDS

To minister effectively to the mentally retarded person, the following items must be considered:

1. SPECIAL CLASSES

The mentally retarded population has unique needs including the necessity for:

- Concrete lessons
- Continual reinforcement
- Repetition
- Consistency
- Individualization
- Instruction in following directions
- Instruction in socialization
- Instruction in self-help skills
- Multisensory teaching techniques

Recommendations:

EMR: The EMR individual should be mainstreamed into a normal classroom *if* he is capable of functioning in that environment. Note that assistants may be needed to ensure individualized instruction.

TMR: Special classes should be created for TMR individuals. However, it is important to mainstream TMRs into other church activities *as much as possible.*

2. TRAINED STAFF

In addition to providing a special class for mentally disabled persons, the teachers and assistants staffing the classes should be trained to develop the following competencies:

- An understanding of God's plan for those with mental disabilities
- A conceptual understanding of the physiological factors that influence learning
- An understanding of learning theory as it relates both to normal children and to mentally retarded persons
- An awareness of existing curricula designed for persons who are mentally retarded
- An understanding of the biblical principles relating to the discipline of children
- An understanding of the biblical principles relating to leadership
- A knowledge of class management procedures

Many people feel that a person must possess "special" qualities in order to work with retarded persons. Any individual, however, who is allowing the Spirit of God to control his life already has these special qualities.

The fruit of the Spirit is love, joy, peace, patience, kindness, goodness, faithfulness, gentleness and self-control (Gal. 5:22–23).

3. CURRICULUM

The dilemma that presents itself to those working with mentally retarded persons of all ages is that most materials simple enough to be comprehended by them are designed for children. Try to imagine a hulking young man of twenty paging through a book illustrated with pictures of Dick and Jane! The image is incongruous.

It is important to provide curriculum materials that will not be demeaning to students. The resources listed at the end of this chapter include materials which have been developed specifically for mentally disabled persons.

4. THE CLASSROOM

The classroom should be:

- Located on the ground floor, since some of the class members will be physically disabled.
- Free from distractions (auditory, visual, etc.).
- Large enough to permit some physical activity.
- Well lighted and attractively decorated.
- Accessible to a drinking fountain and rest rooms.
- Equipped with open shelves, cupboards, and bins for an assortment of toys, books, papers, crayons, and puzzles, as well as chalkboards, flannel boards, bulletin boards, and varying sizes of chairs and tables to accommodate the persons who will remain in the class from year to year.

5. MINISTRY

It is important to provide opportunities for mentally retarded persons to become involved in Christian service. This will give them a sense of personal worth and recognition. In addition, they will be performing worthwhile tasks for their church, which might include:

- Folding Sunday bulletins
- Stuffing envelopes
- Setting up chairs
- Mowing lawns

In general, mentally retarded individuals excel at routine, repetitive tasks.

RESOURCES

General Insights

Brightman, Alan. *Like Me.* Boston: Little, Brown, 1976.

Clark, D.; Dahl, J.; and Gonzenbach, L. *Look at Me, Please Look at Me.* Elgin, Ill.: David C. Cook, 1973.

Hawley, Gloria H. *Laura's Psalm.* Grand Rapids: Zondervan, Impact Books, 1981.

Perske, Robert. *Circles of Friends.* Nashville: Abingdon, 1988.

————. *Hope for the Families.* Nashville: Abingdon, 1981.

Special Education Leadership (magazine). 127 Ninth Avenue North, Nashville, TN 37234.

"What Everyone Should Know About Mental Retardation" (pamphlet). Available from:

Mississippi Association for Retarded Citizens
813 West Pine Street
Hattiesburg, MS 39401

For In-Depth Study

Ebersole, M.; Kephart, N. C.; and Ebersole, J. B. *Steps to Achievement for the Slow Learner.* Columbus, Ohio: Charles E. Merrill, 1968.

Kirk, Samuel A. *Educating Exceptional Children.* Boston: Houghton Mifflin, 1972.

Koch, Richard, and Dobson, J., eds. *The Mentally Retarded Child and His Family: A Multidisciplinary Handbook.* Seattle: Bruner/Mazel, 1970.

Monat, Rosalynn K. *Sexuality and the Mentally Retarded: A Clinical and Therapeutic Guidebook.* San Diego: College Hill, 1982.

Nabi, Gene. *Ministering to Persons With Mental Retardation and Their Families.* Nashville: Convention Press, 1985.

Oosgerveen, G., and Cook, B. *Serving Mentally Impaired People: A Resource Guide for Pastors and Church Workers.* Elgin, Ill.: David C. Cook, 1983.

Resources Related to Christian Education for Mentally Retarded Persons

Bogardus, La Donna. *Christian Education for Retarded Persons.* Nashville: Abingdon, 1969.

Clark, D.; Dahl, J.; and Gonzenbach, L. *Teach Me, Please Teach Me.* Elgin, Ill.: David C. Cook, 1974.

Esmeier, James F. *Materials and Methods for Teaching Mentally Retarded Children*. Watertown, Wis.: Bethesda Lutheran Home, n.d.

Groenke, P. H. *Bringing the Mentally Retarded to Their Savior*. Watertown, Wis.: Bethesda Lutheran Home, n.d.

Hahn, H. R., and Raasch, W. H. *Helping the Retarded to Know God*. Concordia Leadership Training Series. St. Louis: Concordia, 1969. Textbook and guide.

Hawley, Gloria H. *How to Teach the Mentally Retarded*. Wheaton, Ill.: Victor, 1978.

Hooten, J. *Happy-Time Course: Leader's Yearbook*. Wheaton, Ill.: Scripture Press, 1977.

Palmer, Charles E. *The Church and the Exceptional Person*. New York: Abingdon, 1961.

Pierson, J., and Korth, R., eds. *Reaching Out to Special People: A Resource for Ministry With Persons Who Have Disabilities*. Cincinnati: Standard, 1989.

Pierson, James. *77 Dynamic Ideas for the Christian Education of the Handicapped*. Cincinnati: Standard, 1977.

Sources of Curricula for Mentally Retarded Persons

Bethesda Lutheran Home
700 Hoffmann Drive
Watertown, WI 53094-6294
(414) 261-3050

Produces film, videotape, and printed materials relating to special education

Concordia Publishing House
3558 South Jefferson Avenue
St. Louis, MO 63118
(314) 268-1000

Produces dated Sunday school curriculum for special education

Friendship Foundation
2850 Kalamazoo Avenue SE
Grand Rapids, MI 49560
(616) 246-0842

"Friendship Series" religious curriculum for persons with mental impairments

Grace Community Church
13248 Roscoe Boulevard
Sun Valley, CA 91352
(818) 782-5920

Teacher training curriculum

Southern Baptist Convention
127 N. Ninth Avenue
Nashville, TN 37234
(800) 458-2772

Special education resource kit and Bible study

Secular Resources

Association for Retarded Citizens, Inc. (ARC)
500 E. Border Street, 3d floor
Arlington, TX 76010
(817) 261-6003

National Down Syndrome Congress
1800 Demster Street
Park Ridge, IL 60068
(800) 232-6372

President's Committee on Mental Retardation
330 Independence Avenue SW
North Building
Washington, DC 20201
(202) 245-7634

Special Olympics International
1350 New York Avenue NW, #500
Washington, DC 20005
(202) 628-3630

U.S. Department of Health and Human Services
Public Health Service
Health Services Administration
Bureau of Community Resources
Rockville, MD 20857
(202) 857-8400

Christian Resources

Bethesda Lutheran Home
    700 Hoffmann Drive
    Watertown, WI 53094-6294
    (414) 261-3050
Christian Reformed Church in North America
    Committee on Disability Concerns
    2850 Kalamazoo Avenue SE
    Grand Rapids, MI 49560
    (616) 246-0837

    Friendship Ministries
    2850 Kalamazoo Avenue SE
    Grand Rapids, MI 49560
    (616) 246-0842
Handi*Vangelism
    Bible Club Movement, Inc.
    237 Fairfield Avenue
    Upper Darby, PA 19082
    (215) 352-7177
National Apostolate with Mentally Retarded Persons
    P.O. Box 4711
    Columbia, SC 29240
    (803) 782-2706
National Christian Resource Center
    700 Hoffmann Drive
    Watertown, WI 53094
    (800) 369-4636
Shepards Home and School
    1805 - 15th Avenue
    Union Grove, WI 53182
    (414) 878-5620
Southern Baptist Convention
    Sunday School Board
    127 North Ninth Avenue
    Nashville, TN 37234
    (615) 251-2772
Task Force on Mental Retardation
    Ministries in Christian Education
    National Council of Churches
    475 Riverside Drive, Room 708
    New York, NY 10115
    (212) 870-2297

When they call me retarded,
That word's all they see.
Sometimes I think,
They don't even see me.

VI

Deafness

A SUNDAY MORNING EXPERIENCE

I attended a worship service today, different from any I had experienced previously. I understood it only through an interpreter for it was conducted in another language. I did not even hear the typical friendly chatter that goes on before a worship service. Yet it was clear that the room was quiet only to me. I watched deaf people in sweet fellowship with each other. I saw a young deaf man step to the front of the church and welcome everyone to the Lord's house, using confident, sweeping signs. He said, "Let us pray," and yet no people closed their eyes or bowed their heads. They watched him sign toward heaven, and their expressions seemed to indicate heartfelt agreement with his prayer. My interpreter spoke to me in English, helping me to appreciate this beautiful, silent, and active communion with God.

A deaf woman stepped up to lead the congregation in songs of praise. She seemed to sign to an inner rhythm, exalting the Lord, as her love for Jesus shone from her eyes. Soon hands throughout the room were moving in unison, glorifying God. Then the deaf pastor walked up with his Bible and began to preach. He did not preach from behind a pulpit, but used the width of the stage, painting pictures with his hands of God's incredible grace and provision for every Christian. I am so grateful I had an interpreter that day, for clearly I was the only one in the room who was handicapped.

To have an effective ministry with deaf people, an important principle must be understood: *The purposes for a deaf ministry must be the same as the purposes of the church.*

As members of the church, we are to worship, witness, have fellowship, grow spiritually, and use our spiritual gifts to serve the body. These are the mandates given to the church; and likewise, these must be the purposes of a deaf ministry.

When we understand this principle, we will have the proper foundation for a deaf ministry. We will view deaf people as ministers of the gospel of Christ and not just objects of ministry. Deaf individuals will be able to teach, preach, lead prayer or praise, and be fully functioning members of the body of Christ.

This chapter presents several models for deaf ministry. As you read this chapter, remember that these models provide different methods to achieve the purposes of the church.

AN UNREACHED PEOPLE GROUP

Jesus has commanded us to "Go and make disciples of all nations" (Matt. 28:19). The word *nations* has been defined as cultural people groups, communities sharing a common language, culture, and worldview. According to this definition, the deaf community is one of the nations to which we are commanded to go.

Dr. Ralph Winter, director of the U.S. Center for World Mission, refers to unreached people groups as "those which do not yet have an indigenous church established." While a small number of deaf churches have been planted and are thriving with completely indigenous leadership, they are rare. The deaf community worldwide is basically an unreached people group.

DESCRIPTION

Definition

The Conference of Executives of the American Schools for the Deaf has defined deaf people as "those who do not have sufficient residual hearing to enable them to understand speech successfully, even with a hearing aid." As is often the case, such a definition does not allow for the inevitable exceptions. There are people who define themselves as deaf and yet have the ability to understand speech within a controlled environment.

Causes

Deafness and varied degrees of hearing impairments are caused by
• Birth defects
• Disease
• Trauma
• Accident
• Aging
Deafness can be hereditary, but this is the exception, not the rule. Most deaf couples will give birth to hearing children.

Classifications

Most educators, audiologists, and pathologists classify people with hearing impairments according to the degree of hearing loss or when the deafness occurred. For example, congenital deafness refers to deafness that occurs at birth, while adventitious deafness refers to loss of hearing sometime after birth.

It is important to note that deaf people use a different means for classifying themselves, and the method is less concerned with the amount of hearing loss one has. DeAnn Sampley, in her book *A Guide to Deaf Ministry*, states:

> There are many subgroups within the deaf community, including prelingual deaf, children of deaf parents, hard-of-hearing people, postlingual deaf, oral deaf, and at times hearing people who work with deaf people (such as teachers, interpreters, and deaf advocacy agency workers).[1]

Misconceptions

There are many myths and misconceptions surrounding people who are deaf. This makes sensitivity a necessity in deaf ministry. It is presumptuous and unethical for one group to impose its needs upon another group. Instead, it is imperative that the individuals be accepted for who they are and that their needs be discovered. Deaf people are not

1. **Mentally retarded** — Deaf persons have normal intellectual capacities; there are deaf lawyers, scientists, actors, doctors, teachers, inventors, and chemists. The educational process for deaf people has often been limited due to the inability of hearing people to accept their deafness and the failure to provide adequate educational opportunities.

2. **Physically disabled** — The reading and writing skills of deaf people span the same range as those in the hearing community. Those with greater educational opportunities would naturally have greater skill.

   It should be noted that a deaf person's intelligence and acquired knowledge should not be measured by his or her English skills. The deaf person's primary language is sign language, which is not related to the written language of a country. A deaf person may be extremely articulate in sign language, but not in the spoken/written language of one's native country. One should not be misled by writing or speech.

   Remember that when deaf persons use English to communicate, they are using their second language.

3. **Hearing** — Often when someone with a disability is encountered, the assumption is that there is a need to "fix it" and make that person as "normal" as possible. One deaf man shared that he spent the majority of his life at the hands of an audiologist, a speech therapist, an ear doctor, and a surgeon. When he was eighteen and his mother realized he was never going to hear or talk, she finally accepted him for who he was.

4. **Deaf and dumb** — Be careful with labels and phrases. The majority of those who are deaf desire to be called Deaf (with a capital *D*); others may wish to be called hearing impaired or hard-of-hearing. "Deaf and dumb" is never the correct terminology. Very

5. Identical

few deaf people are truly mute. They laugh and shout and can often make audible sounds. While it is true that many deaf people share similar values, language, and culture, they are nevertheless individuals. They have their own needs and as much individuality as any other people group. There are deaf people who are intense, and those who are comical. Some are very lonely; others have many friends. There are both followers and leaders in the deaf community.

DEAF MINISTRY

Introduction

Throughout history, the education of deaf people has been a controversial issue. In the United States, Thomas Gallaudet, who has been called "the father of deaf education," developed a method of educating deaf persons so they could learn to read the Bible. Gallaudet advocated the use of sign language. Subsequently many schools for deaf people were established, a movement gradually developed, and deaf men and women had an opportunity to assume leadership roles in American society.

Then in the late 1800s, at the Milan Conference in Italy, hearing educators announced their support of a method of education called "oralism." Under this program deaf people were to be taught to speak and to read lips, and sign language was to be discouraged. The idea was to make deaf people as "normal" as possible. In time, the oral method not only proved to be unsuccessful, but also erected barriers that kept deaf men and women from assuming leadership roles.

In recent decades other methods were introduced, and the battle continues. Some argue in support of mainstreaming deaf persons—that is, integrating deaf children into hearing classrooms and programs through interpreters. Others advocate deaf schools and specialized programs to ensure that deaf students have equal opportunities in education and recreation.

Often the church's approach to deaf people in its midst has paralleled the philosophies of deaf education. Early in the history of Christian education in the United States, deaf Christian men, like circuit riders, traveled by train or horse to reach other deaf people and teach the Bible. Small groups of deaf Christians began to meet in various cities. While they were not called "churches," they functioned as bodies of believers and began to develop indigenous forms of worship. Then a new form of ministry swept the United States, and hearing churches began to provide interpreters. Deaf people were thereby integrated into the worship services of hearing congregations.

Today Christians are accepting the concept of the deaf church with renewed interest and zeal. Deaf persons are being equipped and are taking the lead in developing Bible study groups and churches that serve the needs of the deaf community indigenously.

It is a great challenge to "go and make disciples." And that is the ultimate goal of deaf ministry. At the same time, deaf persons need to be equipped to reach others for Jesus Christ.

Preparing for Ministry

When starting a ministry, it is important to be sensitive to the needs of the community and to select the most appropriate model. But before the model can be determined, the people who are to be involved in the ministry must be adequately prepared.

FIRST STEP: A WILLING HEART

The first requirement for developing a deaf ministry is a willing heart. The Bible speaks of the need for this attitude:

> Acknowledge the God of your father, and serve him with wholehearted devotion and with a willing mind, for the LORD searches every heart and understands every motive behind the thoughts (1 Chron. 28:9).

> For the eyes of the LORD range throughout the earth to strengthen those whose hearts are fully committed to him (2 Chron. 16:9).

SECOND STEP: TO LEARN OR NOT TO LEARN SIGN LANGUAGE

Before outsiders can enter into a group, be accepted, and be able to share the gospel, they must take time to learn the language and culture of the group.

So is learning sign language essential for everyone involved in a disability ministry? Naturally, to work directly with deaf people requires knowing sign language. But in the church setting, not knowing the language should not be a deterrent to developing deaf ministry. Ministry with those who are deaf can use hearing workers in many different ways, depending on their skills and spiritual gifts. If you are gifted in administering programs and desire to begin a deaf ministry, recruit dedicated ministry leaders who do know sign language.

Successful deaf ministries have begun with people who had no knowledge of sign language. If your vision for ministry is from the Lord, he will provide interpreters.

It is important to spend time with deaf people. Begin by praying for a humble attitude of respect, a commitment to reaching deaf people with the love of Jesus, persistence in learning sign language, a desire to minister with deaf individuals, and the ability to encourage deaf brothers and sisters to reach others for Christ.

THIRD STEP: TARGET THE PEOPLE GROUP AND ITS NEEDS

Although it is not possible to categorize all deaf people, most of them fall into one of three classifications.

Deaf Cultural Group

Deaf people who consider themselves members of the deaf community or cultural group were born deaf or became deaf usually before the age of five. This identification includes embracing and being an advocate for their native sign language (American Sign Language/ASL). Indeed, language is a major factor in distinguishing cultural groups.

The deaf persons in this group have probably attended a deaf residential school or a public school that has a deaf program.

The degree of hearing loss has no effect on whether they consider themselves a part of the deaf community. They may be profoundly deaf or hard-of-hearing, but they make an active choice to identify with the deaf community.

This group can best be served by our providing opportunities for service, fellowship, spiritual growth (including leadership training), and most specifically, by providing deaf worship services. The deaf church model, discussed later in this chapter, provides deaf people with comprehensive Christian ministry.

Deaf or Hearing Impaired

Many deaf and hearing-impaired people do not view themselves as belonging to a cultural group. These people usually desire to function within the hearing community. They may become deaf as children and never learned sign language because of their facility with English. They may have only a partial loss of hearing and define themselves as hard-of-hearing. They may have been raised by the oral method of education and learned to speak at a functional level.

Many people in this category choose to learn sign language in early adulthood and become a part of the deaf community. Some who do not learn sign language, however, may search for belonging, not identifying with either the deaf or the hearing world. Special sensitivity and insight are required to minister effectively to these individuals.

Ministry to this specific group will include both interpreters for those with severe hearing loss and amplification for those with partial loss of hearing. Providing fellowship and barrier-free worship and events will meet needs within this group. Transportation may also be a key need—a need that can be met by people not skilled in ASL.

Deafened Adult

People who lose hearing during or after school age constitute another category. Their culture is the hearing culture even though their ears have become deaf. They will generally go through a process of grieving the loss of their hearing, in contrast with those who do not remember ever having been able to hear. These deafened adults do not usually learn sign language, and they may feel isolated. Consequently, they may require some special support.

The needs of this group are quite different from the needs of those who grew up deaf. These people will require special assistance. They may need sign language training or persons to assist them by taking notes. Again, some in this group may require amplification. According to the specific case, both oral and sign interpreters may be necessary.

FOURTH STEP: DETERMINE YOUR MINISTRY MODEL

After you have carefully studied the needs of deaf persons in your community, you will need to determine what type of ministry would be most appropriate. We offer three models.

Models for Ministry

THE DEAF CHURCH MODEL

This church is a unique ministry, not part of another church. It will achieve the purposes of a church and have the characteristics of a church by itself.

Bible Study. Begin to develop a deaf church by establishing a Bible study. Structure the Bible study in a way that conduces and supports the language and culture of deaf persons.

Deaf people have jokingly said that hearing Bible study teachers are known for their opening jokes, three points, a poem and a summary, while deaf teachers are known for their introduction, story, one point, an application, and plenty of interaction.

Visual aids such as pictures are especially effective for instruction. Allow adequate time for fellowship beforehand, and afterward for interaction regarding the information learned. The interaction can be planned, as in role-playing or small-group discussions.

Location: (1) Sharing a location: Many churches with hearing members begin a deaf Bible study group, using the facilities and resources of the established church. This is often helpful when hearing members participate in nondeaf worship and programs; (2) providing a separate location: Deaf people may resist meeting in a facility already used by hearing people. Some are fearful of facing the kind of discrimination that they have experienced in the workplace. It may prove to be a more effective outreach to begin a Bible study or church in a home, a deaf club, or a community center.

Leadership. The presence of strong deaf leadership is important. All leadership should be fluent in the native sign language while also exhibiting spiritual maturity as recorded in 1 Timothy 3 and Titus 1. These leaders will serve as role models to the entire deaf community.

THE DEAF DEPARTMENT MODEL

The church with a deaf department seeks to make its ministry and programs fully accessible to deaf people.

Individualized Ministry Plans

Develop a written ministry plan for each deaf adult or child. Leadership should discuss with the deaf person and his or her family their specific needs. Determine the interests of the deaf person, then seek to schedule interpreters for those programs.

Trained Interpreters

It has been said that a truly accessible program requires two sign interpreters for every four deaf persons. This seems more idealistic than realistic, yet the interpreter's role is vital to facilitating communication between a speaker and deaf persons. Therefore the placement of interpreters in all-important. The interpreter should stand or sit in a place designated by the deaf people. Interpreters should alternate about every twenty minutes; this enables them to provide quality signing and protects the interpreters from fatigue or nerve damage.

THE MINISTRY ASSISTANCE MODEL

Determine whether a deaf person in the church or the community has specific needs, and plan a program to meet those needs. These questions will help you explore the needs:

- If the deaf person does not know sign language, would it be helpful to enlist a notetaker?
- Would additional sound amplification be helpful?
- If the deaf person depends on reading lips, is the seating arrangement adequate?
- Would an oral interpreter be of benefit?
- If the deaf person has visual impairment, is special interpretation needed?
- Does the deaf person use a sign code system different from sign language, requiring a special interpreter?

Ministry Hints

A Guide to Deaf Ministry by DeAnn Sampley offers the following hints on what to do and what not to do in relating to deaf people:[2]

- **Do not** use the phrase "deaf mute" or "deaf and dumb." The correct terms are "deaf," "hard-of-hearing," or "hearing impaired." **Do** ask the deaf person which term he or she prefers. Consider deaf pride.
- **Do not** talk fast, mumble, or shout. Such speech doesn't help. **Do** carry a small pad and pencil in case communication becomes frustrating or for writing down pertinent information.
- **Do not** cover your face with your hands or objects. **Do** maintain eye contact with the deaf person to whom you are talking. Let his or her eyes and face speak to you, and let your face be expressive. Overcome your inhibitions and let your face and body communicate.
- **Do not** allow others to interrupt when you are conversing with a deaf person. This is common etiquette that hearing people tend to forget. If you talk with a deaf person with the help of an interpreter, **do** talk directly to the deaf person; **do not** talk toward the interpreter. Avoid saying to the interpreter, "Tell the deaf person. . . ." (This is a good exercise for role-playing.)
- **Do not** pretend to understand when you don't. Swallow your pride and shake your head "no." **Do** ask the deaf

person to repeat the statement or to write it down. Otherwise you could find yourself in an embarrassing situation.

- **Do not** ignore a deaf person who is present in a group of hearing people. **Do** include the deaf person as much as possible in the conversation.
- **Do not** correct a deaf person's English unless he or she asks for help.
- **Do not** let fear of making mistakes in sign language keep you from approaching a deaf person. If you can't sign, face the deaf person directly and speak slowly, but not in an exaggerated fashion. (It is helpful if beards and mustaches are well trimmed so as not to obscure the lips.)
- **Do not** use puns or idioms unless you know that the deaf person has a good command of the English language. But **do** include deaf people when telling jokes; otherwise they may think you are laughing at them. Be sensitive to their feelings.
- **Do not** single out a person because you find his or her deafness a novelty. Treat a deaf person as you would a hearing person. **Do** share the attitudes, desires, and interests you have in common. Establish a friendship because of commonalities, not because of the disability.
- **Do not** throw a wad of paper or another object to attract a deaf person's attention. **Do** tap him or her on the shoulder or wave your hand. In large groups you may flick the lights on and off.

Be sure to involve the deaf people in all the aspects of church life such as skits, Sunday school lessons, special events, and social gatherings. Allow deaf people to usher or to serve Communion—even to lead in prayer along with an interpreter. Every bit of exposure the deaf members receive will in turn help to educate the church body. Remember that deaf people have the same needs as others—a sense that they are respected as whole persons, leaders, and communicators. There is no better place to gain this sense of self-esteem than in the church.

A FINAL NOTE

A ministry to deaf people can be exciting and rewarding. It need not be overwhelming or intimidating. The intent in presenting this material is to acquaint the reader with the deaf culture and with the needs of hearing-impaired persons.

If you are interested in working with the deaf community, become a student of deaf culture. A basic knowledge of this community and culture is essential. This ministry is a cross-cultural experience. DeAnn Sampley's book *A Guide to Deaf Ministry* is a good place to begin.

RESOURCES

General Insights

Ogden, Paul, and Lipsett, Suzanne. *The Silent Garden: Understanding the Hearing-Impaired Child.* Chicago: Contemporary Books, 1983.

Pentz, C. M. *Ministry to the Deaf.* Wheaton, Ill.: Tyndale House, 1978.

Rolfsrud, E. N. *One to One: Communicating the Gospel to the Deaf and Blind.* Minneapolis: Augsburg, 1961.

Yount, W. R. *I Can't/I'll Try.* Falls Church, Va.: 1978. Order from:

William R. Yount
403 Maple Street, Apt. 201
Falls Church, VA 22046

————. *Be Opened! An Introduction to Ministry With the Deaf.* Nashville: Broadman, 1976.

For In-Depth Study

Humphries, T., and Padden, C. *Deaf in America: Voices from a Culture.* Cambridge: Harvard University Press, 1988.

Jacobs, Leo M. *A Deaf Adult Speaks Out.* 2nd ed. Washington: Gallaudet College Press, 1981.

Mindel, E., and Vernar, M. *They Grow in Silence.* Silver Springs, Md.: National Association of the Deaf, n.d.

Sacks, Oliver. *Seeing Voices: A Journey into the World of the Deaf.* Berkeley: University of California Press, 1989.

Sauter, Mark. *Planting Deaf Churches.* Order from:

Deaf Opportunity Outreach
P.O. Box 3999
Louisville, KY 40201

Resources Related to Christian Education for Deaf Persons

Bearden, C., and Potter, J. *Manual of Religious Signs.* Atlanta: Home Mission Board of the Southern Baptist Convention, 1973.

Catalog of Bible Visuals for the Deaf. Order from:

Deaf Missions
R.R. 2
Council Bluffs, IA 51501

Edgar, Lawrence. *Sign Language Made Simple.* Springfield, Mo.: Gospel Publishing House, 1979.

O'Rourke, Terrence J. *A Basic Course in Manual Communication.* Silver Springs, Md.: National Association of the Deaf, 1973.

Riekehof, Lottie L. *The Joy of Signing.* Springfield, Mo.: Gospel Publishing House, 1978.

Sampley, DeAnn. *A Guide to Deaf Ministry: Let's Sign Worthy of the Lord.* Grand Rapids: Zondervan, 1990.

————. "A Guide to Deaf Ministry" (videotape). Council Bluffs, Iowa: Deaf Missions, 1989.

Secular Resources

Alexander Graham Bell Association for the Deaf
    3417 Volta Place NW
    Washington, DC 20007-2778
    (202) 337-5220 Voice/TDD

Deafness Research Foundation
    9 East 38th Street
    New York, NY 10016
    (212) 684-6556 Voice
    (212) 684-6559 TDD

Gallaudet University
    800 Florida Avenue NE

Washington, DC 20002-3695
(202) 651-5051 Voice
(202) 651-5052 TDD

National Association of the Deaf
814 Thayer Avenue
Silver Springs, MD 20910
(301) 587-1788 Voice/TDD

Christian Resources

American Bible Society
1865 Broadway
New York, NY 10023
(212) 581-7400

American Missions to the Deaf
7564 Brown's Mill Road
Kauffman Station
Chambersburg, PA 17201
(717) 375-2610 Voice/TDD

Deaf Missions
R.R. 2, Box 26
Council Bluffs, IA 51503
(712) 322-5493 Voice/TDD

Deaf Opportunity Outreach (D.O.O.R.)
P.O. Box 1327
Louisville, KY 40201
(502) 635-1700

Deaf Video Communications of America, Inc.
4624 Yackley Avenue
Lisle, IL 60532
(708) 964-0909 TTY

Evangelical Lutheran Church in America
Disability Ministries
8765 West Higgins Road
Chicago, IL 60631
(312) 380-2692

Gospel Ministries for the Deaf
4200-A S.E. Jennings Avenue
Portland, OR 97267
(503) 393-5153

Lutheran Church–Missouri Synod
    Ministry to the Deaf
    1333 South Kirkwood Road
    St. Louis, MO 63122
    (314) 965-9917, ext. 321

Southern Baptist Convention
    Deaf Ministries
    1350 Spring Street NW
    Atlanta, GA 30367
    (404) 898-7303 Voice
    (404) 898-7395 TDD

Task Force on the Hearing Impaired
    Ministries in Christian Education
    National Council of Churches of Christ
    475 Riverside Drive
    New York, NY 10115
    (212) 870-2297

United Methodist Church
    Ministries With the Deaf
    475 Riverside Drive, Room 350
    New York, NY 10115
    (212) 870-3870

Telecommunications Device Information

Harris Communications
    3255 Hennepin Avenue, Suite 55
    Minneapolis, MN 55408
    (800) 825-6758 Voice/TDD

Telecommunications for the Deaf, Inc.
    814 Thayer Avenue
    Silver Spring, MD 20910
    (301) 589-3043

Weitbrecht Communications, Inc.
    2656 29th Street, Suite 205
    Santa Monica, CA 90405
    (213) 452-8613 Voice
    (213) 452-5460 TDD

Accept to Understand

We know and see each other with blinders on
Boys and girls, men and women
Orange hair, white skin, funny speech, hurt faces.
And we write each other off because "they" aren't like us.
"Oh yes, come in and have a chair
But don't think you are one of us.
We'll tease you, laugh at you and put a name on everyone."
"Eunice is afraid."
"Tim is mouthy."
"Laura is pretty."
"Jack is thoughtful."
But what if I have all four traits
Have equal parts of fear, mouthiness, good looks
*   and intelligence*
What will you name me then?
Who are you to decide what I am?
Just accept me for what I am and take me into your
*   understanding.*
How can we learn each other without being friends?

John Hunt Kinnaird

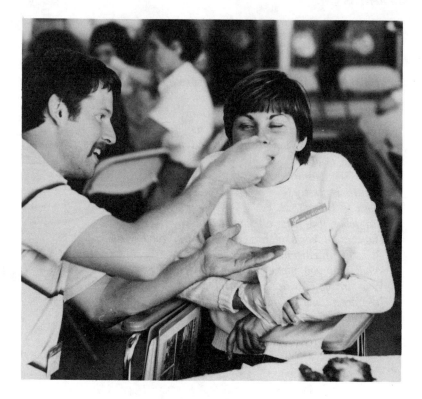

These seminar participants are learning that understanding some of the difficulties encountered by disabled persons is essential for ministering to them. Photo used by permission of JAF Ministries.

VII

Physical Disabilities

To keep me from becoming conceited . . . there was given me a thorn in my flesh, a messenger of Satan, to torment me. Three times I pleaded with the Lord to take it away from me. But he said to me, "My grace is sufficient for you, for my power is made perfect in weakness" (2 Cor. 12:7–9).

Scholars disagree as to the exact nature of the "thorn" that the apostle Paul describes in his second letter to the Corinthians, though most assume that Paul was referring to a physical affliction of some kind.

Thorns come in different sizes and shapes, from the seemingly harmless prick of myopia (nearsightedness) to the devastating wound of severe disability. Every person who has ever lived has felt the sting of a thorn. Yet God's children have his promise of sufficient grace to conquer any trial they may face.

DESCRIPTION

Definition

Physical disability results from a neurological impairment (such as cerebral palsy or epilepsy), an orthopedic impairment (such as brittle bones or arthritis), or other health impairments (such as heart disease or asthma). The degree of involvement ranges from problems of minimal discomfort to severe, debilitating conditions that interfere with a person's ability to function normally.

Causes

Physical handicaps result from
• Birth defects
• Disease
• Accidents

Statistics

Approximately 13 percent of the population of the United States has some degree of physical disability.[1]

Misconceptions

Not only do those who are physically disabled have to endure the pain and discomfort of their illness or ailment, but they must also deal with many popular misconceptions. It is necessary to emphasize that physically disabled persons *are not*

1. **Mentally retarded**	Although some have the dual problems of physical disability and mental retardation, the majority have perfectly normal intelligence.
2. **Deaf**	Physically disabled people usually possess normal hearing. *Do not yell.*
3. **Emotionally unstable**	Physically disabled people have the same emotional needs as those who do not have physical disabilities.
4. **Uncomfortable when talking about their disabilities**	A disability need not be ignored or denied between friends; however, until you establish a friendship, show interest in him or her as a person apart from the disability.
5. **Unlovable**	Disabled people are just as capable of expressing love as people who are not disabled; *however*, when a person is bitter, he or she may appear to be unlovable or incapable of

loving. That person needs to be reminded that because of God's great love for us, there is not only provision for eternal life with him, but a unique plan for each individual in *this* life.

6. **Unfriendly**   A physical disability may result in poor self-esteem leading to withdrawal from friends and associates. That person needs to experience unconditional Christian love in order to learn that God's love is not contingent on outward appearances.

7. **Failures**   Physically disabled persons have been successful in many walks of life, including politics, business, and athletics.

DON'TS

When working with physically disabled persons, it is important that you consider the following suggestions:

DON'T ...

... Pity them.   Uninformed people often pity those with disabilities, but disabled persons need love, understanding, friendship, and encouragement—not pity.

... Stare.   People who stare at a disabled person are forgetting that he or she has real feelings and needs. Instead, try a warm smile or initiate friendly conversation.

... Do everything for them.   Encourage a sense of self-sufficiency in disabled persons by letting them do as much as possible for themselves. Stand by to offer any assistance that is needed. Then depend on your disabled friends to let you know when it is appropriate for you to step in and lend a hand.

... Be impatient.   A person with certain physical disabilities may require more time in moving from place to place or in completing sentences. Allow the disabled person to set the pace.

. . . Ignore them.	Always acknowledge the presence of a disabled person. Attempt to include him or her in your conversation.
. . . Pretend to understand.	If you cannot understand what a person is trying to communicate, ask him to repeat, and listen carefully.
. . . Be afraid to talk.	Though communication with a disabled person is sometimes difficult, demonstrating the love of God through friendly concern will overcome all obstacles.
. . . Be afraid to touch.	The sense of touch—a pat on the back, a handshake, a warm hug—speaks volumes and assures physically disabled people that you do not consider them "untouchable."
. . . Be afraid to correct.	When working with young people, you can expect the same behavior from disabled persons as from any other group of the same age. Firm and loving discipline will let them know that you do not see their "differences."
. . . Talk baby talk.	Physically disabled people possess normal intelligence and resent others talking down to them.
. . . Stereotype them.	Remember that people with physical disabilities are, first of all, people. Do not think of them as labels—cerebral palsy, polio, muscular dystrophy, etc.

ACCEPTANCE

In 1 Corinthians 12:7, the apostle Paul writes, "Now to each one the manifestation of the Spirit is given for the common good." Two important principles are stated in this passage:

1. Every believer has a spiritual gift.
2. Spiritual gifts are intended for building up the body of Christ.

From this passage we can conclude that disabled persons must be given an opportunity to use their spiritual gifts. If churches will encourage the disability community to this end, two objectives will be achieved:

1. The disability population will develop a sense of self-worth as they contribute to the life of the church.
2. The body of Christ will be built up.

Even the most severely disabled person can contribute by

- Praying
- Caring
- Listening
- Being wise
- Being happy
- Maintaining a spirit of optimism and joy

As a leader you must help those with physical disabilities discover their gifts, encourage them to use these gifts, and then commend them when they have edified the congregation.

NEEDS

At first glance, people typically tend to focus on the most obvious differences between themselves and those with physical disabilities. Actually, when we come to know them better, it is soon evident that their needs are similar to our own. Physically disabled people need love, fellowship, instruction in the Word, an opportunity to worship, and an opportunity to minister their spiritual gifts. They are more like us than unlike us! Therefore it is important to integrate them into the mainstream of church life as much as possible.

There is neither Jew nor Greek, slave nor free, male nor female, for you are all one in Christ Jesus (Gal. 3:28).

Listed below are some special needs of physically disabled persons that should be accommodated, whenever possible, in a manner that will not tend to separate these brothers and sisters from other members of the body.

1. **Barrier-free access**   The physical church structure may be designed or adapted so that it is accessible to handicapped members. (See "Resources Re-

lated to Barrier-free Environment" at the end of this chapter.)

2. **Special ministry assistants** Trained assistants should be available for such tasks as pushing wheelchairs, toileting, communicating, etc. (See chapter 10 for suggested skills needed by assistants.)

3. **Equipment** A tape-lending library can be very useful for physically disabled persons. Adjustable tables and ramps may also be needed to accommodate wheelchairs.

4. **Transportation** Many physically disabled persons will need transportation to worship services, Bible study, and church activities. (See chapter 10.)

DISABILITIES

NAME	DESCRIPTION	CHARACTERISTICS
Amputation	Surgical: removal of diseased limb Congenital: limb missing from birth	Lack of function or mobility due to missing limb
Arthritis	Inflammation of joint	Limited movement at affected joint
Arthrogryposis	Persistent contracture of a muscle	Loss of mobility in affected joint
Cerebral palsy	Paralysis, weakness, or general incoordination due to brain damage	Increased muscle tone, uncontrolled movements, often accompanied by mental retardation
Cleft palate	Congenital fissure in roof of mouth, forming passageway between mouth and nasal cavities	Speech defect
Congenital anomalies	Term given to a divergency present at birth	Vary, depending on nature of anomaly
Cystic fibrosis	Respiratory and digestive system malfunction	Medication and inhalation therapy necessary to aid breathing and digestive processes

NAME	DESCRIPTION	CHARACTERISTICS
Diabetes mellitus	Inability to metabolize carbohydrates	Medication may be required. Often a diabetic needs to eat every two or three hours
Down syndrome	Genetic defect that causes mental retardation and various physical defects	Short stature, speech impairments, oriental-looking eyes
Encephalitis	Inflammation of the brain	Can cause brain damage
Epilepsy	Neurological disorder	Various forms of seizures that may cause unconscious and uncontrolled movements
Erythroblastosis (Rh disease)	Blood disease: destruction of red blood cells. A common cause of mental retardation	A transfusion at birth can remedy the defect. If not treated, brain damage can result
Hemophilia	Blood disease: poor clotting ability	Minor scrape or bruise can result in severe hemorrhage
Hydrocephalus	Increased accumulation of cerebrospinal fluid in ventricles of brain	Large head, usually accompanied by mental retardation
Legg-Perthes disease	Degeneration of hip joint	Special brace offers excellent chances for recovery
Multiple sclerosis	Gradual degeneration of nerve pathways to muscles	Numbness, vertigo, gradual loss of muscle function
Muscular dystrophy	Progressive degeneration of voluntary muscle functions	Frequent falling, waddling gait, difficulty climbing stairs, gradual loss of strength until walking becomes impossible
Osteogenesis imperfecta	Brittle bones	Minor fall can result in broken bones
Poliomyelitis	Contagious disease caused by virus that attacks the gray matter of spinal cord	Possible paralysis
Rheumatic fever	Inflammation of heart, joints, brain, or all of these	Heart damage

NAME	DESCRIPTION	CHARACTERISTICS
Shunt	Anomalous passage or one artificially constructed to divert flow from one main route to another	
Spina bifida	Incompletely formed spinal cord	Paralysis, muscle weakness, and loss of sensation
Spinal cord injury	Trauma to spinal cord	Paralysis
Stoma	Artificially created opening between two passages or body cavities, or between a cavity or passage and the body's surface	Usually an external bag to collect body wastes

RESOURCES

General Insights

Eareckson, Joni. *Joni.* Grand Rapids: Zondervan, 1976.

Eareckson, Joni, and Estes, Steve. *A Step Further.* Grand Rapids: Zondervan, 1978.

Headlines. A magazine regarding brain injury; available from:

New Medico Publishing
14 Central Avenue
Lynn, MA 01901
(800) CARE TBI, ext. 3002

Krauss, B. *An Exceptional View of Life: The Easter Seal Story.* Norfolk Island, Australia: Island Heritage, 1977. Now available from the National Easter Seal Society (see address under "Secular Resources").

Kreyer, V. "The Physically Handicapped Person: An Area of the Church's and Minister's Responsibility." *Pastoral Psychology* 16 (1965): 5–7.

————. "Feelings of Handicapped Individuals." *Pastoral Psychology* 16 (1965): 41–44.

Sheetz, T. *Bringing Christ to the Handicapped.* Upper Darby, Pa.: Handi*Vangelism, n.d. Order from:

Handi*Vangelism
237 Fairfield Avenue
Upper Darby, PA 19082
(215) 352-7177

Singleton, Bev, and Tada, Joni Eareckson. *Friendship Unlimited.* Wheaton, Ill.: Harold Shaw, 1987.

Spinal Network. Newsletter available from:

Spinal Associates, Ltd.
P.O. Box 4162
Boulder, CO 80306
(800) 338-5412

Wheeler, Bonnie. *Challenged Parenting.* Ventura, Calif.: Regal, 1983.

For In-Depth Study

Cook, Rosemarie S. *Counseling Families of Children With Disabilities.* Dallas: Word, 1990.

Kirk, Samuel A. *Educating Exceptional Children.* Boston: Houghton Mifflin, 1972.

Mount, B., and Zwernik, K. "It's Never Too Early, It's Never Too Late." A booklet available from:

Metropolitan Council
Mears Park Center
230 East Fifth Street
St. Paul, MN 55101
(612) 291-6359

Seinkiewicz-Mercer, R., and Kaplan, S. *I Raise My Eyes to Say Yes.* Boston: Houghton Mifflin, 1989.

Vanier, Jean. *The Broken Body.* Mahwah, N.J.: Paulist, 1988.

Resources Related to Barrier-free Environment

Access: A Bibliography of Resources Related to Barrier-free Environment. New York: National Council of Churches, 1978. Order from:

National Council of Churches
Ministries in Christian Education
475 Riverside Drive

New York, NY 10115
(212) 870-2297

Architectural and Transportation Barriers Compliance Board
1111 18th Street NW, Suite 501
Washington, DC 20036-3894
(800) 872-2253

Secular Resources

American Amputee Foundation
2506 Riverfront Drive #3
Little Rock, AR 72202
(501) 666-2523

Council for Exceptional Children
1920 Association Drive
Reston, VA 22091-1589
(703) 620-3660

Epilepsy Foundation of America
4351 Garden City Drive
Landover, MD 20785
(301) 459-3700

The Library of Congress
Division for the Blind and Physically Handicapped
1291 Taylor Street NW
Washington, DC 20542
(202) 707-5100

Muscular Dystrophy Association
3561 East Sunrise Drive
Tucson, AZ 85718
(602) 529-2000

National Easter Seal Society
70 East Lake Street
Chicago, IL 60601
(312) 726-6200

National Multiple Sclerosis Society
205 East 42nd Street, 3d floor
New York, NY 10017
(212) 986-3240

National Organization for Rare Disorders
P.O. Box 8923

100 Route 37 Fairwood Professional Building
New Fairfield, CT 06812-1783
(800) 447-6673

National Spinal Cord Injury Association
600 West Cummings Park, #2000
Woburn, MA 01801
(800) 962-9629

Spina Bifida Association of America
1700 Rockville Pike, #540
Rockville, MD 20852
(301) 770-7222

United Cerebral Palsy Association, Inc.
66 East 34th Street
New York, NY 10016
(212) 481-6300

Christian Resources

Assemblies of God
Handicapped Ministries
1445 Boonville Avenue
Springfield, MO 65802
(417) 862-2781

Christian and Missionary Alliance
Office of Special Ministries
P.O. Box 35000
Colorado Springs, CO 80935-3500
(719) 599-5999

Christian Council on Persons With Disabilities
P.O. Box 458
Lake Geneva, WI 53147

Christian Overcomers
246A Third Avenue
Westwood, NJ 07675
(201) 358-0055

Episcopal Diocese of Minnesota
Ministry With Persons Who Are Handicapped
3225 East Minnehaha Parkway
Minneapolis, MN 55417
(612) 871-5311

Evangelical Lutheran Church in America
    Disability Ministries
    8765 West Higgins Road
    Chicago, IL 60631
    (312) 380-2692

Handicaps for Christ Crusade
    6427 Scottsville
    Wichita, KS 67219
    (316) 721-2900

Handi*Vangelism
    237 Fairfield Avenue
    Upper Darby, PA 19082
    (215) 352-7177

JAF Ministries
    P.O. Box 3333
    Agoura Hills, CA 91301
    (818) 707-5664

Share, Care and Prayer (environmental illness support)
    905 North First Avenue
    Arcadia, CA 91006
    (818) 446-2609

Southern Baptist Convention
    Ministry to the Disabled
    1350 Spring Street NW
    Atlanta, GA 30367
    (404) 898-7438

United Methodist Church
    475 Riverside Drive, Room 350
    New York, NY 10115
    (212) 870-3870

VIII

Visual Impairments

BURDEN OR BLESSING?

The campfire had nearly consumed its supply of fuel. Only the luminous embers could be seen in stark contrast to the black of the night. The silence was occasionally interrupted by testimonies of praise from the campers:

"I thank God for the mountains."
"I thank God for loving us."
"I thank God for the fun day."

Suddenly a small voice rang out. "I thank God that I am blind. I will never see the filth of the world. The first thing my virgin eyes will ever see is the shining face of Jesus."

Implicit in that potent testimony is the hope of everlasting life and an imperfect body made perfect for eternity.

Roger Dyer, executive director of the Christian Fellowship for the Blind, has stated:

> Blindness is what you make it—a burden or a blessing. It can be a lifetime spent in self-pity and an eternity of darkness as well, or it can be the challenge of a lifetime, to fulfill your greatest physical potential in spite of the odds; and it can be the beginning of the greatest spiritual adventure of your life—and it can last for eternity. Christ has made it possible.[1]

Blindness can indeed be a blessing; however, for that to occur, the loss of vision must be replaced by the "Light of the World," the Lord Jesus Christ.

DESCRIPTION

Definition

A person is said to be "legally blind" if his or her central visual acuity does not exceed 20/200 in the better eye with correcting lenses, or the visual field is less than an angle of twenty degrees.

In simpler terms, a person is considered legally blind if he or she can see no more at a distance of twenty feet than someone with normal vision can see at a distance of two hundred feet.

Causes

The eye is much like a camera. Light passes through the clear cornea, the aqueous humor (a watery liquid), the opening in the iris called the pupil, and finally through the lens and vitreous, which focuses the image on the retina. The retina transmits the image to the brain as a nerve impulse.

There are four major eye diseases. Each disease affects a different part of the organ.

DISEASE	PART OF EYE AFFECTED	DESCRIPTION
Glaucoma	Aqueous humor	Obstruction to the circulation of the aqueous humor
Cataract	Lens	Clouding of lens
Macular degeneration	Retina	Central visual acuity affected
Diabetes	Blood vessels of retina	Hemorrhaging inside eye

Classifications

Visual impairments are divided into two categories:

1. **No sight**   No optic impulses received by brain

2. **Partial sight,** including—
   - Blurry vision   Vision of 20/200 or worse
   - Spotty vision   Caused by scars on retina
   - Night blindness   A condition in which an individual cannot see well in a faint light or at night
   - Tunnel vision   Peripheral vision limited to 20 degrees or less

STATISTICS

It is estimated there are about 11.4 million persons in the United States with some kind of visual impairment; that is, persons who have trouble seeing even with corrective lenses. Of these, 3.1 million are severely impaired. This means either they are "legally blind" or they function as such. About 627,400 are "legally blind," while 140,000 people have no usable vision at all.[2]

It is noteworthy that about one-half of the "legally blind" persons in the United States are over sixty-five years of age. This is because the diseases that are the primary causes of blindness in this country are usually associated with aging.

DON'TS

When working with visually impaired individuals, consider these suggestions:

DON'T . . .

> . . . treat the blind person as if he or she were retarded. Most blind persons have normal intelligence and will comprehend what you are saying.
>
> . . . yell! Visually impaired people have problems with sight, not hearing.
>
> . . . be overly helpful. The blind person is inconvenienced, not incapacitated. With minor adaptations, those who are blind can participate in most activities.

   . . . address a blind person through an intermediary. If you want to ask a question, ask the person directly.

   . . . make unusual revisions in conversation, such as substituting the word *heard* for the word *see.*

   . . . pet a dog guide without the owner's permission.

HINTS

The following hints will enable you to minister more effectively to those with visual impairments:

1. Offer   It is always appropriate to offer assistance. However, do not be surprised if a blind person prefers to try most things himself.

2. Ask   If you are eager to help a blind person but are not sure exactly what to do, don't hesitate to ask how you can be most helpful.

3. Touch   A gentle touch on the elbow is the best way to get a blind person's attention.

4. Lead   If a blind person gives you permission to walk with him, do not grab his arm—let him take yours. He may want to walk a half-step behind you. From the motion of your body, he or she will be able to tell when you come to curbs, steps, or turns.

5. Announce   When you enter a room or area where a blind person is present, make it a point to speak to him or her as soon as possible.

6. Orientate   When a blind person changes environments (during a walk, for example), be sure to inform him or her of obstacles, inclines, or slippery or uneven surfaces.

7. Adapt   The visually impaired person will be able to compensate for the loss of sight if activities, lessons, etc., are adapted.

8. Teach   When explaining a concept to a blind person, use concrete examples and incorporate or refer to as many of the other senses as possible.

9. Stimulate   Humor and voice inflection are important when speaking with a blind person. These techniques will help to set the mood and will compensate in some measure for the lack of visual stimuli.

NEEDS

People with visual impairment have unique needs. With a little imagination and minor adaptations, however, a visually impaired person can participate in most church activities. Several factors must be considered to accommodate visually impaired people, as follows.

1. PHYSICAL PLANT

These modifications in construction will enable a church to meet the needs of people who are visually impaired:

Handrails   Handrails are imperative with all stairs.

Guides   For carpeted areas, end the carpeting two steps short of the stairway to serve as a warning to blind persons that they are approaching stairs.

Lighting   Some visually impaired persons have limited sight. For these, proper lighting is essential. For example, there should be adequate light at book level in all pews. Remember that glare causes eye fatigue much more quickly in poorly sighted persons. Therefore, areas surrounding the preacher or speaker should be illuminated with soft, glare-free light.

(For more detailed information, see the resource list on barrier-free environment at the end of this chapter.)

2. CURRICULUM

Sunday school quarterlies, Christian books, and Bibles for those who are blind are available from various sources. (See Christian education resources listed at the end of this chapter.) Consider these guidelines for using various types of materials:

Large print   Many visually impaired persons can read large print (18-point type is the accepted size for legally blind people). Various materials are available in large print. However, materials not available in large print can be developed by using 18-point type on nonglare paper. Some copy machines have the capacity to enlarge print materials.

Braille
Some visually impaired people prefer Braille as their primary reading method. Many denominations produce materials such as Sunday school lessons and hymnals in Braille.

Tapes
Some visually impaired people can read neither large print nor Braille. Generally this group comprises persons who have lost their sight later in life or are otherwise physically disabled. Although tape recordings are popular with all visually impaired people, they are especially helpful for this group. Major denominations have tapes available through lending libraries. Tapes of local church services can also be easily produced by volunteers; they are inexpensive to make, do not require special equipment, and can be developed relatively quickly.

Other materials
The use of concrete examples is vital to the learning process. People learn through experience; therefore, multisensory teaching techniques will promote optimal learning, especially with children. In the absence of the visual sense, it is important that blind children be encouraged to use all available sensory means to learning. Examples:

Finger paints	Modeling clay
Salt and flour	Papier-maché
Mosaics	Collages
Drama	Handling of animals
Puppetry	

3. PRINT ACCOMMODATIONS

Generally, people with visual impairments will be easily assimilated into the church body. Some accommodation is necessary, however, for them to make use of printed materials such as hymnals, Bibles, Sunday school curriculum, church bulletins, and posted information. Many denominations and Christian bookstores have some materials available in large print or on cassette. Braille materials are not as prevalent, although some denominations do provide them. Resources for materials are listed at the end of this chapter.

Because Bibles on cassette do not contain chapter and verse references, lesson materials recorded on tape should include all the Scripture verses read in full. Braille Bibles are extremely bulky, filling as many as thirty-two volumes, so many Braille readers prefer materials on tape.

Church volunteers can help by taping materials or offering to read bulletin board announcements, newsletters, and personal mail. They also can offer to take notes during worship services and classes or to write personal correspondence.

Volunteers are needed for visually impaired children in their classes, especially when a class is working on arts and crafts.

4. TRANSPORTATION AND MOBILITY

Transportation and moving about in a crowded environment can be challenging for a visually impaired person. The church that is sincerely interested in ministering to these people will arrange reliable transportation to all church activities.

There are simple ways to provide this kind of help. Volunteers can assist at buffet lines by carrying trays, negotiating crowded areas, or locating rest rooms. Asking the person with a visual impairment to join you during a worship service, then assisting as needed, is a good way to start a friendship.

5. MINISTRY

There are few ministries that are limited to sighted people. Therefore it is important to encourage a blind person to become actively involved in service at the church. Counseling, evangelism, teaching, and prayer are just a few of the kinds of ministries available to those with visual impairments.

RESOURCES

General Insights

Kerr, J. S. "The Visually Handicapped: Our Blind Spot." *Spectrum* 49 (1973): 25–28.

Publications available from the American Foundation for the Blind (AFB), 15 West 16th Street, New York, NY 10011:

Corn, A. L. *Are You Really Blind?* New York: AFB, 1985.

Dickman, I. R. *Making Life More Livable.* New York: AFB, 1983.

Grayson, D. *Facts About Blindness and Visual Impairment.* New York: AFB, 1981.

Reihl, D. E. *Molasses, Feathers and Eggshells: Craft Activities for Blind, Visually Impaired and Multihandicapped Children.* New York: AFB, 1985.

Tannenbaum, R. A. *A Different Way of Seeing.* New York: AFB, 1984.

In-Depth Study

Kemper, R. C. *An Elephant's Ballet: The Story of One Man's Successful Struggle With Sudden Blindness.* New York: Seabury, 1977.

Publications available from the American Foundation for the Blind (AFB), 15 West 16th Street, New York, NY 10011:

Carroll, Thomas. *Blindness: What It Is, What It Does, and How to Live With It.* Boston: Little, Brown, 1985.

Corn, A., and Martiniez, I. *When You Have a Visually Handicapped Child in Your Classroom: Suggestions for Teachers.* New York: AFB, 1977.

Resources for Barrier-free Environment

Environmental Modifications for the Visually Impaired. A handbook available from:

Committee on Architectural and Environmental Concerns
of the Visually Impaired
2454 Salem Place
Fullerton, CA 92635

Resources in Christian Education for Visually Impaired Persons (See also "Christian Resources")

Duckert, M. *Open Education Goes to Church.* Philadelphia: Westminster, 1976.

Maxson, B. J. "A Blind Child in My Sunday School Class . . . ?"
Starkville, Miss.: CARE Ministries, 1990. Available from:

CARE MINISTRIES, Inc.
218 Louisville Street
Starkville, MS 39759
(601) 323-4999

Tobey, K. *Learning and Teaching Through the Senses.* Philadelphia:
Westminster, 1970.

John Milton Sunday School Quarterly. Biblical studies in Braille, based on
the Uniform International Sunday School Lessons with notes and
illustrative materials, published four times a year. Available from:

The John Milton Society for the Blind
475 Riverside Drive, Room 832
New York, NY 10115
(212) 870-3335

Radiant Life Series. Available in Braille and on cassette from:

Assemblies of God
1445 Boonville Avenue
Springfield, MO 65802
(417) 862-2781

Resource Kit: Persons With Visual Handicaps and the Church. Available
from:

National Council of Churches
Ministries in Christian Education
475 Riverside Drive
New York, NY 10115
(212) 870-2297

The Secret Place. A daily devotional guide in Braille. Available from:

Periodical Distribution
American Baptist Churches
P.O. Box 851
Valley Forge, PA 19482
(800) 458-3766

Sunday school materials for blind people, available from:

Christian Education for the Blind, Inc.
P.O. Box 6399
Fort Worth, TX 76115
(817) 923-0603

The Upper Room. A daily devotional guide available in large print, Braille, and cassette editions. Available from:

The Upper Room
1908 Grand Avenue
Nashville, TN 37203
(615) 340-7200

Secular Resources

American Council of the Blind
    1155 15th Street NW, Suite 270
    Washington, DC 20005
    (202) 424-8666
    (800) 424-8666

American Foundation for the Blind
    15 West 16th Street
    New York, NY 10011
    (212) 620-2000
    (800) 232-5463

American Printing House for the Blind
    P.O. Box 6085
    Louisville, KY 40206-0085
    (502) 895-2405

Blind Children's Fund
    230 Central Street
    Auburndale, MA 02166-2399
    (617) 332-4014

Clovernook Center
    Rehabilitation and Employment Center
    7000 Hamilton Avenue
    Cincinnati, OH 45231
    (513) 522-3860

National Association of Parents of the Visually Impaired
    2180 Linway Drive
    Beloit, WI 53511-2720
    (800) 562-6265

National Federation of the Blind
    1800 Johnson Street
    Baltimore, MD 21230
    (800) 638-7518

Recording for the Blind, Inc.
20 Roszel Road
Princeton, NJ 08540
(609) 452-0606
(800) 221-4792

United States Association of Blind Athletes
4708 46th Street NW
Washington, DC 20016
(202) 393-3666

Christian Resources

Assemblies of God
Ministries to the Blind
1445 Boonville Avenue
Springfield, MO 65802
(417) 862-2781

Bible Alliance
P.O. Box 621
Bradenton, FL 34206
(813) 748-3031

Bibles for the Blind and Visually Handicapped International
3408 Rosehill Road
Terre Haute, IN 47805
(812) 466-4899

Braille Circulating Library
2700 Stuart Avenue
Richmond, VA 23220
(804) 359-3743

CARE Ministries
218 Louisville Road
Starkville, MS 39759
(800) 336-2232

Christian Mission for the Sightless, Inc.
5450 Boy Scout Road
Lawrence, IN 46226
(317) 549-2386

Christian Record Services
4444 South 52nd Street

Lincoln, NE 68506
(402) 488-0981

Clearer Vision Ministries
P.O. Box 570268
Orlando, FL 32857-0268
(407) 381-1373

Eyes of Faith Ministries, Inc.
P.O. Box 743336
Dallas, TX 75374-3336
(214) 669-1103

Evangelical Lutheran Church in America
Braille and Tape Service
426 South 5th Street, Box 1209
Minneapolis, MN 55440
(612) 330-3502

Lutheran Braille Evangelism Association
660 East Montanta Avenue
St. Paul, MN 55106
(612) 776-8430

Mark II Ministries
P.O. Box 30286
Indianapolis, IN 46320
(317) 253-5971

National Church Conference of the Blind
P.O. Box 63
Denver, CO 80201
(303) 455-3440

Southern Baptist Convention
Ministry to the Disabled
1350 Spring Street NW
Atlanta, GA 30367
(404) 898-7438

United Methodist Church
Ministries With the Blind
475 Riverside Drive, Room 350
New York, NY 10115
(212) 870-3870

Photo used by permission of JAF Ministries.

Jesus loves me
This I know
For the Bidle
Tellz me so

IX

Learning Disabilities

I CAN'T

Robert Carpenter tells about a boy named Billy in his book *Why Can't I Learn?*

Two anxious parents leaned forward in their chairs one day in the principal's office of a suburban elementary school and listened hopefully as the school psychologist outlined a remedy for Billy, their third-grader. Halfway through, the principal interrupted.

"I'm sorry," he said, "but we've tried that already, and it doesn't work in this case."

Little Billy was not learning in spite of a good IQ, a good school, an involved teacher, a concerned principal and dedicated but frustrated parents. The dilemma was regrettably familiar: "We've done this before; it's not the answer."

The principal suggested Billy's parents take him for a physical checkup, only to be told by the doctor their child was healthy and would probably "grow out of his problem."

The parents next arranged for private tutoring. They obtained the counsel of several other child psychologists recommended by the school who attempted to establish better understanding between child and parents. These sessions served to ease the tension that exists when children who have the ability to learn do not live up to parental expectations.

And yet, despite all these efforts, Billy's attitude improved only slightly, thus aiding the behavioral aspect of the problem, but his learning disability remained unchanged.

Family after family hears the verdict: "The problem is that we've done this before, but it's not the answer. Something is missing." The acknowledgment of an unresolved problem is at least a step toward solution.

The problem is not borne only by parents. Children who suffer learning disabilities inwardly yearn just as intensely and even more so for success. They are frequently misunderstood when they use unacceptable, and sometimes destructive, attention-getting devices. Such negative compensating adjustments are cries for help caused by frustrating problems of underachievement in education.[1]

This story is not at all uncommon. People like Billy are found in all strata of society—across all economic and ethnic lines.

DESCRIPTION

Definition

A learning disability refers to a specific disorder in one or more of the processes of speech, language, perception, behavior, reading, spelling, writing, or arithmetic.

In other words, children are classified as having a "learning disability" when (1) they have trouble learning, (2) their learning problem is not the result of a disability such as deafness, blindness, or mental retardation, or (3) they show highs and lows in different areas of abilities.

Learning disabilities include conditions that have been referred to as

- Perceptual handicaps
- Brain injury
- Minimal brain dysfunction
- Dyslexia
- Developmental aphasia
- Central processing dysfunctions

Statistics

Learning disabilities affect 4.5 percent of the school population in the United States.[2]

CHARACTERISTICS

The term "learning disability" is a label which encompasses a multiplicity of learning problems. It is important to understand that learning disabilities will differ among individuals. The following are offered as general characteristics:

1. **Normal intelligence**	The individual with a learning disability will usually have average to above-average intelligence.
2. **Diversity of abilities**	The child will have discrepancies in his own mental development, with areas of strength as well as areas of deficiency.
3. **Essential learning processes affected**	One or more of the essential learning processes—perception, integration, expression—are involved.
4. **Identification due to educational disabilities**	Identification is not usually based on overt physical or sensory characteristics, but rather on educational deficits; however, subtle sensory or neurological problems may exist.

NEEDS

There are varying degrees of severity in learning disabilities; consequently, there will be a vast range of abilities and needs. Communication skills, academic potential, and occupational potential will vary from child to child.

Because most children with learning disabilities have normal or above-normal intelligence, their academic potential is generally good. The teacher working with them will need to adapt lessons so that each child can learn according to his or her particular learning pattern. The following guidelines are important to consider:

1. EVALUATION

The learning-disabled person must be evaluated to discover his or her optimal learning pattern. Testing will reveal the child's strengths and weaknesses in visual, auditory, and tactile modes of learning. It will also determine the student's learning potential in contrast to his academic performance.

2. LEARNING STRATEGY

A learning strategy built on the information obtained through the evaluation should be developed for each child. (The information may be available through the child's parents or school.) The evaluation will reveal the "intact modalities" (most efficient sense avenues) and "deficit modalities" (less efficient sense avenues) of the child.

The principle presentation of information should be made through the intact modalities, with the deficit modalities used to complement them. For example, if a child has a strong visual modality but a weak auditory modality, the primary teaching technique should be the use of visual aids, with teaching tools involving sound used to complement the visual instruction.

3. SELF-ESTEEM

The child with a learning disability is very often aware of the fact that he or she is not able to meet the expectations of parents and teachers, resulting in low self-esteem. The following suggestions will aid in instilling confidence and a sense of self-worth in the child:

Praise   Take advantage of every opportunity to praise the child.

Teach   Tell the child that he was uniquely created by God and that God does not make mistakes. In addition, God loves him so much that he sent Jesus to die for him.

Provide   Develop lessons which will permit the child to be success-ful. Goals should be set in light of the child's abilities.

Watch   Be sensitive to the climate in the classroom. Do not allow other children to tease the learning-disabled child.

For more in-depth study on dealing with self-esteem in children, read *Hide or Seek* by James Dobson (Old Tappan, N.J.: Fleming H. Revell, rev. ed. 1983).

4. CLASSROOM

The classroom environment will influence the child with a learning disability. Strive to create an attractive and stimulating environment, using pictures, charts, and visual stimuli.

5. CURRICULUM

Most Sunday school curricula are geared toward persons who are not disabled, while Special Education materials are developed with public school subject matter in mind. It is possible, however, to adapt the applicable Special Education methodologies to the spiritual training of children.

6. INTEGRATION

Children with learning disabilities can be integrated into regular Sunday school classes with some planning and forethought. Train a Special Education assistant to help the teacher in adapting lessons and individualizing instruction.

7. MINISTRY

It is important to involve learning-disabled persons in a ministry appropriate to their skills and gifts. Serving in some way will promote the development of a positive self-image.

RESOURCES

General Insights

Evans, James S. *An Uncommon Gift*. Philadelphia: Westminster, 1983.

Hill, Charles. Various articles on learning disabilities, available from:

Learning With
2900 Queen Lane
Philadelphia, PA 19129

"Learning Disabled Children: Who Are They?" (November 1973).

"If Your Child Has a Learning Disability" (December 1973).

"The Learning Disabled Child Goes to Church School" (January 1974).

"Treating Learning Disabilities" (February 1974).

"Discipline—A Matter of Attention" (September 1974).

————. "Diagnosis: Learning Disability." *The Christian Home* (1974). Available from:

The Christian Home
201 Eighth Avenue South
Nashville, TN 37202

Jean, Priscilla. "Who Is the Child With a Learning Disability?" *The Christian Home* (1973). See preceding entry for address.

Levine, Mel. *Keeping a Head in School: A Student's Book About Learning Abilities and Learning Disorders.* Rev. ed. Cambridge, Mass.: Educators Publishing Service, 1991.

Stevens, Suzanne H. *The Learning Disabled Child: Ways That Parents Can Help.* Winston-Salem, N.C.: John F. Blair, 1980.

————. *Classroom Success for the Learning Disabled.* Winston-Salem, N.C.: John F. Blair, 1984.

Van der Stoel, Saskia, ed. *Parents on Dyslexia.* New York: Taylor & Francis/Multilingual Matters, 1987.

For In-Depth Study

Carpenter, Robert D. *Why Can't I Learn?* Glendale, Calif.: Gospel Light, 1974. Also available from the author:

R. D. C. Publishers
4741 School Street
Yorba Linda, CA 92686.

Journal of Learning Disabilities. Pro-Ed Journals, 8700 Shoal Creek Boulevard, Austin, TX 78758-6897.

Lerner, Janet W. *Children With Learning Disabilities.* Boston: Houghton Mifflin, 1989.

Silver, Archie, and Hagin, Rosa. *Disorders of Learning in Childhood.* New York: John Wiley, 1990.

Resources in Christian Education for People With Learning Disabilities

Weiss, M., and Weiss, H. *A Parents and Teachers Guide to Learning Disabilities: A Practical Guide to Activities Which Interest and Instruct Youngsters.* Yorktown Heights, N.Y.: Board of Cooperational Educational Services, n.d.

Secular Resources

Academic Therapy Publishers
20 Commercial Boulevard
Novato, CA 94947
(415) 883-3314

Council for Exceptional Children
Division for Children With Learning Disabilities
1920 Association Drive
Reston, VA 22091-1589
(703) 620-3660

HEATH Resource Center
One Dupont Circle NW, Suite 800
Washington, DC 20036
(202) 939-9320

The Learning Disabilities Association
4156 Library Road
Pittsburgh, PA 15234
(412) 341-1515

National Center for Learning Disabilities
99 Park Avenue, 6th Floor
New York, NY 10116
(212) 687-7211

National Dyslexia Referral Center
P.O. Box 781532
Dallas, TX 75378
(214) 350-0033

National Network of Learning Disabled Adults
800 North 82d Street, Suite F2
Scottsdale, AZ 85257
(602) 941-5112

Orton Dyslexia Society
   Chester Building, Suite 382
   8600 LaSalle Road
   Baltimore, MD 21204
   (301) 296-0232
   (800) 222-3123

Christian Resources

National Institute for Learning Disabilities
   107 Seekel Street
   Norfolk, VA 23505
   (804) 423-8646

Talent Night

Jesus gives all of us things we can do.
    Stand on your head
    Play a horn or piano
I know a man who can make up skits.
And also some girls who can sing.
    I love to see you do what you do.
    I do my thing too.

John Hunt Kinnaird

Photo used by permission of JAF Ministries.

X
Getting Started

A TEN-STEP PLAN FOR SUCCESS

In launching a disability ministry you will want to ask yourself some planning questions and have an idea of what you want to accomplish. A good planning exercise will help you define goals, train teachers and workers, establish adequate emergency procedures, resolve logistical problems, and in general give your ministry tracks to follow. We suggest an easy-to-follow, ten-step planning process.

1. BEGIN WITH A VISION AND PRAYER

Seek the Lord to learn his desire for disability ministry in your church.

The first and most important step is prayer—relying on God for his leading. Any new ministry must begin with prayer. J. Oswald Sanders has said:

Since leadership is the ability to move and influence people, the spiritual leader will be alert to discover the most effective way of doing this. . . .

To move men, the leader must be able to move God, for He has made it clear that He moves them through the prayers of the intercessor.[1]

People are wise to plan their steps, but seeking God's direction is necessary for a viable ministry to persons with disabilities. You would also be wise to recruit others to help you seek the Lord's leading. Ask a mature Christian to commit to praying with you and for you. Then be accountable to the Lord and your prayer partner for your attitudes and actions.

2. CONTACT CHURCH LEADERS

Share with your pastor or elder(s) your heart and desire for ministry. Present a general "game plan" for the ministry.

Pastoral and elder support is crucial. In their book *Strategy for Living*, Edward R. Dayton and Ted W. Engstrom state:

> Planning helps us move toward goals, but planning helps in many other ways as well. Planning is a way of communicating our intentions to ourselves and to others. "Do two walk together unless they have agreed to do so?" (Amos 3:3). Unless you have decided where you are going, how can I decide to accompany you?[2]

Your desire and preparation will go a long way in attaining support from church leaders. Seek their input and prayers for ministry development. In addition to being accountable to the Lord and your prayer partner, you are also accountable to your church leaders as ministry develops.

3. DETERMINE A TARGET POPULATION

Establish a target population—that is, what type(s) of disabilities, what age participants—the ministry will serve.

In all likelihood you will not be able to "do it all." Not only are disability groups varied, but you and your volunteers can probably best serve a defined group—at least, at the outset. Pray about your desire, and plan your ministry around the needs you have assessed and the talents available.

A good way to obtain information about the need for such a ministry is through a church survey. Because 10 to 15 percent of the population has some degree of disability, it is very likely that the same percentage of your congregation are either disabled or associated with people who are.

4. IDENTIFY AND BRIDGE BARRIERS

Make your church accessible in architecture, attitude, and communication.

Attitude and communication are important issues. The involvement of church leaders is imperative at this point. Pastors can lend support through sermons, or the church can sponsor a Disability Awareness Sunday.

Educating the congregation about disability will cause fears and misunderstandings to diminish.

Along with attitudinal barriers, disabled people must overcome physical barriers. Physical accessibility consists of ramps, adequate rest rooms, parking spaces, and—if necessary—elevators. The free publication *The Uniform Federal Accessibility Standards (UFAS)* is available from the Architectural and Transportation Barriers Compliance Board, 1111 18th Street NW, Suite 501, Washington, DC 20036-3894.

5. DEFINE A PHILOSOPHY, PURPOSE, AND GOALS

Develop the philosophy of the church's ministry, state the purpose, then set both long-term and short-term goals.

The place to begin is to determine a philosophy that includes all the groups to whom you desire to minister, both adults and children.

A. OVERALL PHILOSOPHY

Scripture expresses the goal of Christian education as a "trained-up" child. The child must reach a state of maturity in which he or she is self-disciplined, acting on the foundation of God's Word (2 Tim. 3:16–17). Ephesians 4:14 says:

Then we will no longer be infants, tossed back and forth by the waves, and blown here and there by every wind of teaching and by the cunning and craftiness of men in their deceitful scheming.

Spiritual growth should be the intent of every Christian education program. People with disabilities do not necessarily need to be segregated. Disabled people should have the same opportunities for learning as their nondisabled friends. At times, disabled individuals need to be mainstreamed (that is, included in regular classes), and at others there should be classes specifically designed around their needs. Sometimes all that is needed is an adaptation of teaching methods to suit the persons with disabilities. Determine what is best for your church and your target group.

B. PURPOSE AND GOALS

To determine the effectiveness of any endeavor, we must set objectives. Dayton and Engstrom state in *Strategy for Living:*

> We need to start with purposes in our lives. We need great visions, grand dreams, great faith. But God expects us to take our faith a step further and set goals—statements that are measurable and accomplishable.
>
> A purpose, then, is an aim or direction, something which we want to achieve, but something which is not necessarily measurable.
>
> A goal, on the other hand, is a future event which we believe is both accomplishable and measurable. Measurable in terms of what is to be done, and how long it takes to do it.[3]

You need, first, to determine the purpose of the ministry. Then specific goals can be written to assist teachers in fulfilling the purpose. Two cautions must be mentioned:

- It takes an experienced teacher to set reasonable goals. If goals are not realized initially, perhaps they were unrealistic. Teachers must continually evaluate their goals and lessons in light of new knowledge and insights.
- Do not, however, become a slave to goals. Goals are merely tools for directing our teaching in pursuit of a purpose. The goals may change altogether or be modified by unforeseen circumstances.

The following examples of purposes and goals will guide you as you create some appropriate for your ministry:

Purposes	Goals
1. To worship through music	By October 20, students will be able to sing three Christian songs.
2. To trust God with problems	By the end of the lesson, students will be able to delineate at least one area of concern in their lives and share that concern with a disability ministry worker.
3. To learn to communicate with God through prayer	By the end of the lesson, when asked to pray, a student will be able to express one item of praise and one request to God.

6. RECRUIT AND TRAIN LEADERS AND VOLUNTEERS

Communicate to the congregation the need for disability ministry and ask them to consider participating in the program. Train volunteers toward a basic understanding of the needs of disabled persons.

A disability ministry cannot be successful without the proper personnel. The following considerations will help in recruiting and training staff:

A. RECRUITMENT

To generate maximum interest in the congregation, combine recruitment efforts with an oral disability ministries presentation. Also use bulletin boards, fliers, and newsletters.

B. QUALIFICATIONS

John 16:13 teaches that one purpose of the indwelling Holy Spirit is to reveal truth to Christians. The implication is obvious: To teach in a Christian environment, a person must be yielded to the Holy Spirit. That condition suggests these qualifications:

- The teacher must have a personal relationship with the Lord Jesus Christ (1 Tim. 4:1; 6:3–4; 2 Tim. 2:2).
- The teacher must manifest a high level of maturity and understanding (Eph. 4:11–17; 1 Tim. 3:6).
- The teacher's life must give evidence of control by the Holy Spirit (1 Cor. 3:1–3; Gal. 5:22–23; Eph. 5:18; 2 Peter 1:5–8).
- The teacher's ministry must manifest the necessary combination of gifts to handle the assigned task (Rom. 13:3–8; 1 Cor. 3:5–9; 12:1–31; 1 Peter 4:10).
- The teacher must prove faithful (2 Tim. 2:2).

This list of qualifications could seem overwhelming, but there are certain to be people in your congregation who possess all these qualifications *along with* a love for people with disabilities. Seek God's will in choosing those who should lead and teach.

Recognize that teachers are not necessarily ready-made. Evaluate the skills and maturity of the candidates, then place them in the right positions. Lead them along as they grow in both ability and spiritual maturity.

C. COMMITMENT

It takes time to become acquainted with the distinctive needs of disabled people. Each is an individual; consequently, each person will have specific physical, social, spiritual, emotional, and learning characteristics. To provide continuity for the students, teachers should be willing to commit to a minimum term of one year.

D. TRAINING

A training program should be developed to equip the workers as follows:

- An understanding of suffering as it relates to God's will
- A philosophy of ministry with disabled persons in the church
- An understanding of the unique needs of the specific group with which the person will be working

- Knowledge of physiological factors that influence learning
- An understanding of learning theory
- Skill in preparing lessons that will promote optimal learning
- An awareness of existing curricula for persons with disabilities
- An understanding of biblical principles regarding discipline
- Knowledge of biblical leadership principles
- An understanding of class management procedures

E. TEACHER-STUDENT RATIO

The number of teachers required to work with disabled persons varies according to the situation. The following ratios are offered as guidelines:

Disability	Acceptable ratio	Ideal ratio
Mentally retarded	3:1	1:1
Physically disabled	2:1	1:1
Deaf	4:1	2:1
Blind	1:1	1:1

F. EMERGENCY PLAN

Because of the high incidence of medical problems associated with handicapping conditions, it is wise to adopt a plan of action for emergencies that may arise while disabled persons are on the church premises.

All leaders and workers should be prepared to handle emergency situations. Communicate the emergency plan to all who will spend a significant amount of time at the church (such as staff members and volunteers). Also, the plan should be posted in strategic locations throughout the building, listing procedures to be followed in the event of an emergency.

In developing the plan, consider the following:

1. **First aid**	A working knowledge of first aid is essential for leaders in "high risk" areas

	of the church such as athletics and special ministries.
2. **Emergency medical release statement**	Keep on file a statement from the parents that gives permission for medical personnel to administer emergency treatment to minors.
3. **Emergency treatment information**	Create a file of hospitals with emergency treatment rooms, doctors and local paramedics, with addresses and telephone numbers, including information about the disabled person's personal physician.

A sample information form and medical release statement appear on pages 135–38.

G. HANDLING DIFFICULTIES IN RECRUITMENT

God will allow the proper leaders and workers to emerge if the ministry is in his will. If potentially qualified leaders do not come forward, it may be concluded that

- It is not the Lord's time for such a ministry, or
- It is not the place for the ministry

If, after much prayer, the need is still perceived, continue to pray about how to proceed. Although the need for disability ministries in churches is very real, a program should not be initiated without proper leadership. Avoid rushing into ministry; await the Lord's timing.

7. DETERMINE CLASSROOM, CURRICULUM, AND TRANSPORTATION NEEDS

If you are not mainstreaming students, determine the size of the room that is needed, including all furnishings and equipment. Find appropriate curricula. Provide a means for the students to get to church.

Once you have evaluated the needs of the students, you can determine the classroom requirements.

Consult the resource lists at the end of other chapters to identify sources of curricula for your target group.

As to transportation, consider the following strategies:

A. INDIVIDUAL MINISTRY

Individual members of the church may offer to use their vehicles to transport students for services and activities. The advantages of this strategy are twofold:

- More people will become aware of and involved in the special needs and rewards of disability ministry
- No capital expenditures are required when personal vehicles are used

The disadvantage in this strategy is that wheelchairs might not fit into some cars. In this case, a large vehicle such as a van may be needed. Nevertheless, with careful planning this strategy can be effective, especially if one church member is willing to serve as a transportation coordinator.

BUS MINISTRY

Many churches have found that the purchase of a bus or van enchances the outreach ministries. Along with the capital expenditures, this strategy requires trained and properly licensed drivers.

The advantages of a bus ministry lie in the ease with which wheelchairs and other special apparatuses may be handled.

The disadvantages must be weighed carefully:

- Maintenance and insurance costs on the bus or van may be high
- Persons who are picked up at the beginning of the route may ride for long periods of time
- The exceptional mode of transportation may foster feelings of separation from the rest of the congregation

8. DEVELOP A BUDGET

Determine financial needs for establishing, supporting, and maintaining the ministry.

Once you have determined the congregation's needs, the available leadership, curriculum and classroom requirements, accessibility, and transportation, you will be prepared to determine the actual costs of the ministry.

A clear line of communication with the church leadership is imperative in assessing the financial requirements. Costs should not become a deterrent; the entire congregation will benefit from a disability ministry.

9. PUBLIC RELATIONS

Inform the community of your program. Seek the help of schools, agencies, churches, and other community resources to help advertise your program.

The following provide good means of publicity:

Congregation	Members can inform friends, relatives, and working colleagues about the program.
Residential facilities	Distribute announcements at residential facilities serving disabled persons.
Schools	Distribute publicity at schools. Local parent-teacher groups may be willing to publicize the program in newsletters.
Governmental agencies	Many state and local government agencies that serve people with disabilities may offer publicity.
Private agencies	Private agencies that serve disabled persons may offer publicity.
Newspapers	Prepare news releases and community calendar information for local newspapers.
Television and radio	Television stations must commit a portion of air time to public service announcements. Radio stations often have community service spots.
Word of mouth	If disabled persons find their spiritual needs satisfied through your ministry, they will tell their friends.

10. KNOW THE PARTICIPANTS

Become acquainted with each participant, obtaining essential personal, medical, and emergency information.

It is important to become acquainted with each new participant. Interview the disabled person and, if possible, a parent or relative before he or she is enrolled. The interview should cover these subjects:

A. **Medical conditions** It is essential to understand the limitations faced by a person with a disability. Some physical conditions require careful monitoring and special handling in emergencies:

- Allergies
- Epilepsy
- Heart disease
- Diabetes
- Brittle bones
- Hemophilia

B. **Medication** Medication should be given as prescribed. It is helpful to keep a chart of the medications and dosages required of people in the program, as well as proper written authorization from the person's doctor allowing staff members to administer medication.

C. **Appliances** Many physically disabled persons must use orthopedic appliances such as wheelchairs, braces, or catheters. It is important to understand the proper use of these devices.

D. **Unusual problems** Be aware of any unusual conditions that may require special attention.

The sample forms on pages 120–23 are good examples of the kind of information you will want to keep on file for disabled people involved in your church's ministry. Teachers and other workers need to have easy access to pertinent medical information. An emergency medical release statement is essential.

At the initial interview, discuss the emergency plan and answer any questions that arise.

GETTING DOWN TO BUSINESS

Getting started is a big task, but these ten steps should help. We—the church—must be about our heavenly Father's business. Statistics show that only 5 percent of churches have an outreach to disabled persons, and 95 percent of the people who have disabilities are not active in any church.[4] Therefore, the "business" is urgent.

Not only do we need to minister to people with disabilities, but the church needs their gifts and talents to enhance the body of Christ. The healing message of Jesus Christ is available to all. May the Lord bless you as you share that message with persons with disabilities, and may your life be greatly enriched in doing so.

A workshop is a useful place to learn to assist disabled persons—and to try to experience what others face in reality daily. Photo used by permission of JAF Ministries.

INTERVIEW FORM

Name: _____ Age: _____

Interviewer's name: _____

Name of parent/guardian: _____

Physical disability: _____

Seizures?   ☐ Yes   ☐ No

    How often? _____ Type: _____

    Helpful hints: _____

	Yes	No		Yes	No
Allergies	☐	☐	Lung condition	☐	☐
Heart condition	☐	☐	Special diet	☐	☐

Please note necessary details pertaining to the above:

_____

_____

_____

Precautions: _____

_____

_____

Medication information: _____

_____

_____

Medication schedule: _____

_____

Special appliances:

☐ Wheelchair   ☐ Crutches   ☐ Hearing aid
☐ Walker   ☐ Braces   ☐ Talking board
☐ Canes   ☐ Eyeglasses   ☐ Other _____

Special care of appliances: _____

_____

_____

Behavior information: _____

_____

_____

_____

Assistance: Does participant need assistance with:

	Yes	No	Comments
Feeding	☐	☐	_____
Dressing	☐	☐	_____
Undressing	☐	☐	_____
Toileting	☐	☐	_____
Braces	☐	☐	_____

Additional information: Yes   No

Does the person fatigue easily?   ☐   ☐
Does the person chill easily?   ☐   ☐

Additional comments: _____

_____

_____

Signatures:

_____   _____   _____

Date   Parent/guardian   Interviewer

SPECIAL MINISTRIES, _____ CHURCH
Emergency Medical Release Form

Name _____ Birthdate _____
        Last   First   Middle

Home address _____ City _____ Zip ___

Father _____ Home phone _____
        Home address _____
        Business address _____
        Phone _____ Work days _____ Hours _____

Mother _____ Home phone _____
        Home address _____
        Business address _____
        Phone _____ Work days _____ Hours _____

In emergency, if parents cannot be reached, notify:
        Name _____ Relationship ___
        Phone _____ Address _____

Disability _____ Seizures _____
        Heart condition ___ Lung condition ___ Allergies _____
        Stoma ___ Catheter ___ Shunt ___ Medication? _____
        Wheelchair ___ Crutches/cane ___ Braces ___ Other ___

Comments _____

Medical Release

    We, the undersigned, parents or legal guardians of _____
a minor, and said minor (if 18 years of age or older), do hereby
authorize any adult person in whose care the said minor has
been entrusted by _____ Church to consent to
any x-ray examination, anesthetic, medical or surgical diagnosis
or treatment, and hospital care to be rendered to said minor
under the general or special supervision and upon the advice of a
physician and surgeon licensed under the provisions of the
Medicine Practice Act and to consent to an x-ray examination,
anesthetic, dental or surgical diagnosis or treatment, and hospital
care to be rendered to aid minor by a dentist licensed under the
provisions of the Dental Practice Act.

It is understood that this authorization is given in advance of any specific diagnosis, treatment, or hospital care being required.

The above authorization is given pursuant to the provisions of the Civil Code of this state, section _____.

Photographic Release

We also give _____ /do not give _____ (initial one) our consent to _____ Church to photograph the above named person and, without limitation, to use such pictures and/or stories in connection with any work of said church and do _____ /do not _____ (initial one) hereby release said church from any claims whatsoever which may arise with regard thereto.

Signature of Parents or Legal Guardians:

Date _____ Signature _____

I have read, understand, and agree with the above statement as it applies to me.

Signature of Participant (18 years or older):

Date _____ Signature _____

Personal Physician _____

Accident/Health Insurance Co. _____
Policy No. _____

This chart suggests needs of persons with various disabilities. A dot is placed in categories where a disability program is recommended. When a category is not marked, we suggest that this disability group be mainstreamed into regular classrooms.

Behavior Disorders	Learning Disabilities	Physically Handicapped	Deaf	Blind	Mentally Handicapped	Program	Category
•	•	•	•		•	Bible Study	Worship/Edification
•			•		•	Sunday School Class	
	•			•		Materials Center	
•	•	•	•	•	•	Special Ministries Assistants	
•	•	•	•		•	Discipleship	
•	•	•	•	•	•	Special Friend Program	Recreation
•			•		•	Camping	
			•	•	•	Special Events	
		•	•		•	Individual and Team Sports	
•		•			•	Respite Care	Family
•	•	•	•	•	•	Family Counseling	
•		•			•	Family Day Outings	
•	•	•	•	•	•	Parent Classes	
		•			•	Institutional Evangelism	Outreach
•		•	•			Vacation Bible School	
		•		•	•	Workshops	Special Education
•	•	•	•		•	Learning Center	
		•				Therapy Center	
					•	School	
		•		•	•	Transportation	Trans.
	•	•		•	•	Residence	Res.

• Family

Notes

Introduction

1. Robert Lovering, *Out of the Ordinary* (Phoenix: ARCS, 1985).

Chapter 1

1. J. I. Packer, *Knowing God* (Downers Grove, Ill.: InterVarsity, 1973), 92.
2. Gloria Hawley, "Gifts of Joy," in *Decision* (April 1978).

Chapter 2

1. Charles Swindoll, *Three Steps Forward, Two Steps Back* (Nashville: Thomas Nelson, 1980).

Chapter 3

1. John MacArthur, Jr., *The Church: The Body of Christ* (Grand Rapids: Zondervan, 1973), 121.
2. Ibid., 121–22.

Chapter 5

1. Based on statistics from *ARC Facts*, newsletter of the Association for Retarded Citizens, Arlington, Texas, March 1987.

Chapter 6

1. DeAnn Sampley, *A Guide to Deaf Ministry* (Grand Rapids: Zondervan, 1989), 29.
2. Adapted from Sampley, *A Guide to Deaf Ministry,* 47–48.

Chapter 7

1. Disability Statistics Program, Berkeley, California, August 1991.

Chapter 8

1. Roger Dyer, "Blindness—What Is It?" Available through Christian Fellowship for the Blind International, Pasadena, California.
2. Statistics from the American Foundation for the Blind, New York City, August 1991.

Chapter 9

1. R. D. Carpenter, *Why Can't I Learn?* (Glendale, Calif.: Regal, 1974), 1.
2. Disability Statistics Program, Berkeley, California, August 1991.

Chapter 10

1. J. Oswald Sanders, *Spiritual Leadership* (Chicago: Moody, 1967), 82, 84.
2. Edward R. Dayton and Ted W. Engstrom, *Strategy for Living* (Glendale, Calif.: Regal, 1976), 94.
3. Dayton and Engstrom, *Strategy for Living,* 49.
4. Statistics from the International Year of Disabled Persons, United Nations, 1981.